Rc

THE MICROGUIDE TO PROCESS AND DECISION MODELING IN BPMN/DMN

THE MICROGUIDE TO PROCESS AND DECISION MODELING IN BPMN/DMN

TOM DEBEVOISE
BLACK PEARL DEVELOPMENT, INCORPORATED

AND

JAMES TAYLOR
DECISION MANAGEMENT SOLUTIONS

CONTRIBUTIONS BY RICK GENEVA
FOREWORD BY JAMES SINUR

ADVANCED COMPONENT RESEARCH, INC.
LEXINGTON, VIRGINIA

The MicroGuide to Process and Decision Modeling in BPMN/DMN

Copyright © 2014 Tom Debevoise and James Taylor

ISBN: 978-1-502-78964-8

Library of Congress Control Number: 2008902478

Editing by Christine Parizo, Christine Parizo Communications

Composition and book design by TIPS Technical Publishing, Inc.

Cover design by 2Faced Design

To Mother

—Tom Debevoise

To the Boys

—James Taylor

CONTENTS

FOREWORD

This micro guide book is a must for any serious process, decision or event practitioner, as it covers the modeling of each of these important tributaries of business action. The writings even consider the deep interaction of these three working together for proper business actions. The book is filled with many visual patterns that are likely to be encountered in the real world that can be leveraged.

Since **events** indicate the patterns that are occurring in the context of business interest, modeling their participation, in context, is a real value. Since **decisions** are involved in determining the best actions to take, modeling their participation in triggering and guiding process actions is essential. Last but not least, this writing handles the depth of normal best practice **processes**.

For organizations that have a planning culture, this book is a bible for combining modeling various interacting models. Even organizations that are dealing with complex emerging conditions and dynamic processes can benefit from model patterns interacting together on the fly. As processes become more goal-driven and emergent, driven by poly analytics and dynamic knowledge pools, the patterns in this book can play a role in more liquid actions based on emerging better practices.

Net; Net: This book will stand the test of time in that it will be germane to most processes

—James Sinur

PREFACE FROM TOM DEBEVOISE

As our digital networks have become ever more integrated into the fabric of our lives, the complexity and the scope of functional requirements have exploded. Where the functions of these applications have many integrations points and must work across numerous roles and participants, business process management (BPM) can be a part of this fabric. Today, we are creating environmental, sensor, and model-driven processes which respond to the weather, markets, electro-mechanical conditions, and human behaviors. Compounding complexity is the expectation is that dispersed, heterogeneous software, from cloud-based, mobile software to firmware for hardware, must be upgraded and maintained.

Working in the fields of solution and application development, I have yearned for techniques that clearly model the complex concepts of this multidimensional fabric. Creating process models is a critical method, yet process thinking alone is insufficient. Adding decision management improves the model by focusing on both the way decisions are made and directing the process that must carry out the decision. Next, event modeling can clarify needs by providing another viewpoint. Working with each of these metaphors, process, decision, and events, can create powerful organizing concepts.

Aware of external events, operational conditions and decisions based impermanent "rules," today's processes can provide the needed dynamic characteristics. From all this, I have learned that a rigid vision of how an application should work is a recipe for failure, even over a short time period. The requirement to "change" the solution, even after the solution is operation is pervasive—change is part of the process.

Within this change process, we want to engage the stakeholders with tools that will change their operations to dynamically adapt to new realities. Stakeholders include owners, experts, and customers. The two modeling notations, the subject of this book, Business Process Model Notation (BPMN) and Decision Model Notation (DMN), are powerful and positive steps in this direction. With these, our business analysts now have a rigorous way to graphically model decisions.

Yet this environment is incomplete—data, a critical aspect of creating executable, must be modeled and connected to our BPMN/DMN models. There are no graphical standards for event modeling, and many believe DMN should have a decision graph notation. And most of today's decision-process-event environment is hampered by unnecessary, tedious technical activities that eliminate the non-technical from the creation process.

I believe that what we are striving for is a business-digital domain that can be symbolically manipulated by knowledgeable stakeholders. I believe BPMN/DMN is a solid step in this direction. Process and Decision Models offer visual details that would be impossible to glean from written business and use cases. Near the end of the book, James and I have described how decision modeling directly contributes to the design requirements of the process. This is just a beginning —new, more concise, and powerful modeling techniques will arise from the developments that we will describe.

ACKNOWLEDGMENTS

First, I must acknowledge James Taylor for contributing his world-class expertise on decision management and his open-minded and creative input into this project. In addition to all these talents, he is a superb author and visionary.

With respect to this aspect of my career, I am truly grateful to the cross-functional, cross-business tribe that is business process management and its close offspring, business rules and now decision management. This especially includes Jim Sinur, George Barlow, Tom Dwyer, Mike Lim, Troy Foster, and Jon Siegel. It has been quite a journey for all of us.

As always, I must acknowledge Barbara Debevoise, my wife, best friend, and manager of Advanced Component Research, Inc. of Lexington, VA, which is the publishing owner of this book.

—Tom Debevoise

Preface from James Taylor

I have been working with Decision Management and Decision Management Systems for well over a decade. In my work with companies adopting decision management, I have designed, written about, reviewed, and used many different products. In recent years, one theme has become increasingly clear as a driver for success. Whether companies are developing packaged decision management systems, adopting business rules, or trying to apply big data and advanced analytics to their business, a thorough understanding of the decisions they are focused on is critical. Clearly identifying the decisions they need to improve to hit their business objectives, understanding how to measure those decisions, and seeing clearly how they want to make those decisions is the difference between success and failure.

This understanding led me to decision modeling and, ultimately, to the Decision Model and Notation standard being finalized by the Object Management Group. Along the way, I have met some great modelers, deep thinkers, and many with long histories in decision modeling and design. When Tom asked me to join him in updating this book to include decision modeling and the Decision Model and Notation (DMN) standard, I was delighted to take this opportunity.

I have found decision modeling to be a powerful technique. When combined with process modeling, it allows for the effective application of business rules and advanced analytic technology, improves the clarity and accuracy of requirements, and results in simpler, smarter, and more agile business processes.

In this book, we have seeded decision modeling concepts and techniques throughout, gradually increasing the level of detail in parallel, with detail being discussed on the process modeling side. This parallelism and the treatment of decisions and processes as peers to be managed simultaneously, is central to our approach. Decision modeling is not something to be "bolted on" to process modeling but something that transforms the way we think about business processes and business events to produce a richer understanding of our businesses.

Why do this now? The new DMN standard is being finalized, expected to be released in late 2014. All the core elements are in place, the critical choices made, and any remaining changes will be minor. The profile of decision modeling has also been rising with the release of software products that support decision modeling, such as my company's DecisionsFirst Modeler, as well as the publication of decision modeling as a technique in the Business Analyst Body of Knowledge® v3. Meanwhile, process modeling is stronger than ever, analytics is a hot topic, and business rules management systems are increasingly common in large organizations. Now, it seemed to us, is the time to bring decision modeling into focus.

ACKNOWLEDGMENTS

First and foremost, I would like to thank Tom Debevoise for approaching me to add DMN to this book. Without his enthusiasm for decision modeling and his willingness to revise his existing material to include decision modeling, this would not have been possible.

My work with decision modeling has been informed greatly by the experience and understanding of all those on the Decision Model and Notation submission and finalization teams. Alan Fish of FICO, Christian de Sainte Marie of IBM, Gary Hallmark of Oracle, Paul Vincent, Larry Goldberg and Barb von Halle of KPI, Prof. Jan Vanthienen of The University of Leuven, and many others have a tremendous depth and breadth of knowledge when it comes to decision modeling (and many other) topics. We have argued, debated, agreed, disagreed, refined, and edited together over the last 18 months or so. Like all standards, the result is not perfect, but I believe we have created a foundation that will work and that adds a great deal to current approaches. I would also like to specifically acknowledge Alan Fish's contribution to my personal understanding of decision modeling and recommend his book, "Knowledge Automation: How to implement Decision Management in Business Processes" (Wiley, 2012).

In parallel with working on the standard, I have been able to return to my roots in developing software tools. Decision Management Solutions has developed and released a software product called DecisionsFirst Modeler that provides a collaborative, cloud-based platform for building decision models. Building this software and using it has informed and changed my approach to decision modeling for the better. Gagan Saxena and Meri Gruber of Decision Management Solutions have been instrumental in this, as has Don Perkins, one of our earliest and most detail-oriented users. The software team (Kapil, Vinayak, Kailash) led by Rishi Argawal have been great to work with and can be justly proud of what we have already done and what we will add to the product moving forward.

Sandy Kemsley, Alan Fish and Gil Ronen all invested time in reviewing early versions of my sections and provided numerous helpful suggestions. Any remaining errors are, of course, my own!

As always, my family's patience as I wrote and edited the book is much appreciated, as is the support of Decision Management Solutions' customers, the users of DecisionsFirst Modeler, and all those who let me bounce ideas off them over the last few years.

—James Taylor

INTRODUCTION

The addition of Decision Model and Notation (DMN) has led the evolution of Business Process Model and Notation (BPMN) 2.0 into an even more powerful and capable tool set. This book covers both specifications and, more importantly, focuses on the shifts we have observed in decision and process modeling. A number of best practices have emerged, creating robust, agile, and traceable solutions.

Process improvement is credited with better understanding, communication, and organization, and process modeling is an important aspect of all these. Awareness of business events and event-driven processing has made for more flexible and dynamic business processes, which are reflected in new process modeling approaches. In the coming chapters, we will learn that decision management and decision modeling are likewise critical, allowing for simpler, smarter, and more agile processes. This book incorporates lessons about decision, event, and process modeling.

The addition of decision modeling not only addresses the importance of decisions but also uncovers critical issues that the process must address to comply with the decision. Decision-driven processes act on the directives of decision logic: decision outputs affect the sequence of things that happen, the paths taken, and who should perform the work. Processes provide critical input into decisions, including data for validation and identification of events or process-relevant conditions. The combination of process and decision modeling is a powerful one.

In the face of new challenges and new approaches, business process modeling has evolved in a number of ways:

- Decision modeling sometimes precedes process modeling by defining input data and business knowledge, which leads to a disciplined coordination of decision outcomes in the subsequent process elements.
- The combination of process and decision modeling helps incorporate visibility and business control at a suitable level for successive layers of business units, from the most global to the most local.
- Because the logic of decisions is moved from a process into decision models, process models are simpler.
- Business events are rapidly recognized and processed by well-defined decisions, and can help define how to respond in real-time and change how processes are structured.
- Decision analytics increasingly act as input to a decision, not simply as measures of the overall process.

In modern process modeling, most scenarios incorporate a mix of metaphors that include processes, decisions, and events.

In some business processes, an operational decision is the controlling factor that drives processes after the starting event or events. This is powerful, as many governments and enterprises are focused on minimizing the event response lag because there is often a scaled financial benefit to faster responses. A growing focus on straight-through processing and therefore on automated decision making, not just automated processes, is likewise raising the visibility of decisions in processes. Developing a decision model provides a detailed, standardized approach that precisely directs the process and creates a new level of traceability. Decision modeling can therefore be considered an organizing principle for designing many business processes. Processes that utilize the architectural approach known as the Internet of Things (IoT) are largely driven by events and event processing. Decisions determine appropriate responses to these events.

Most process modeling in BPMN is accomplished by matching a use case, written or otherwise, with workflow patterns. Process modeling is critical to the creation of a robust and sustainable solution. Without decision modeling, however, such an approach can result in decision logic becoming a sequence of gateways and conditions such that the decision remains hidden and scattered among the process steps. Without decision modeling, critical decisions, such as how to source a requisition when financial or counter-party risk is unacceptable, or what to offer a customer, are lost to the details of the process. When the time comes to change or improve a decision, a process model in BPMN alone might not meet the need. Providing a notation for modeling decisions separately from processes is the objective of DMN.

A new perspective on process modeling is reflected in the combination of three ideas—Process, Decision, and Event:

- **Process:** A process can be defined as an organization of activities that happen in a series, relevant to business goals and objectives. At a fundamental level, a process model represents a single instance of a process. That is, the properly designed purchase order process reflects the handling of a single purchase order, rather than the entire organization's method for processing all of its purchase orders.
- **Decision:** All activities and responses to events should be the result of a conscious decision by the organization. Decisions are the result of applying business knowledge to an assemblage of data, either data input to the decision or data that result from precursor decisions. A decision model likewise reflects how a decision is made about a single purchase order. This knowledge is often expressed as business rules.
- **Event:** A process can also be considered a connected sequence of events that respond to states, causes, and conditions. In an event-based view, the process is a linkage of the transitions from one processing state to another. Business events arise from the world outside of the enterprise, as opposed to internal events such as key clicks or transactions. The incorporation of external business events is increasing in modern process modeling.

Each of these perspectives increases the visibility of the overall process model and its underlying logic. A process model is not a standalone scenario; it is a scenario that exists within the context of the business model of the organization and its decisions and events. All of these different perspectives are incorporated appropriately into a robust process model.

One objective of this book is to provide concrete examples of things encountered in process modeling that are matched to these perspectives.

The combination of BPMN and DMN is central for modern process modeling across these perspectives. With BPMN's and DMN's simple visualizations and problem solving techniques, it is easy to create modern, optimized (or at least optimizable) process models.

CHAPTER 1

DEFINITIONS

To create proper models in BPMN and DMN (BPMN/DMN), a grasp of the basic concepts for business process management (BPM), decision management and business event management is needed. Without this, users often create vague, or, in a best-case scenario, workflow-style diagrams with BPMN. They place rules into a nest of gateways or skip over how decisions are being made completely. They fail to account for more interrupt-driven, event-centric scenarios.

In this chapter we will introduce the core definitions for business process management, decision management and business event management.

BUSINESS PROCESS DEFINITIONS

As James Chang[1] has pointed out, traditional or functional work management suffers from a lack of end-to-end focus. A business process is a sequence of activities that achieve a business goal. There are several viewpoints of what a process actually is. The simplest to understand is the traditional process viewpoint:

> *A business process is an organized, coordinated flow of activities, conducted by participants, acting on and deciding with data and knowledge, to achieve a business goal.*

This definition arises from a compendium of BPM literature. It concisely defines:

- The start and end states of process design.
- The design choices of BPMN shapes.

---

1. James Chang, Business Process Management Systems: Strategy and Implementation, Auerbach Publications September 9, 2005,

- The role of decisions.
- Knowledge-based control of process relationships with economic conditions, perhaps with analytics.

The essential points of business processes are illustrated in Figure 1.1 below:

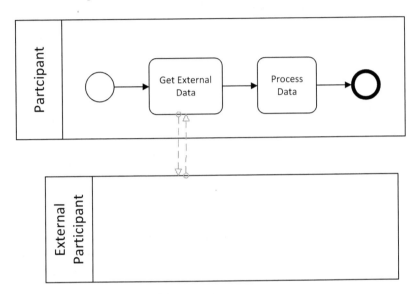

Figure 1.1 *A simple process model in BPMN.*

- An event (shown by a circle) is a message, indicator, announcement, or a point in time that is created internally or externally by the organization.
- A flow (shown by lines and arrows) is the movement of data from shape to shape. There are two types of flows in a business process: a sequence and a message. Flows can move from event to event, activity to activity, and activity to event.
- An activity (shown by a rounded rectangle) is a task that is performed by a process participant.
- A participant (shown by a horizontal or vertical lane) is any resource that is involved in a business process e.g., a single person, a group of people, a system, or another process.

Not shown in this example process model are:

- Data consisting of structured information that is owned by a business process. The BPMN specification includes data as inputs and outputs for processes and activities. Business processes can also pass on or transmit and alter unstructured documents.

- The specific decision-making approach required for any activity that requires a decision to be made. This would be modeled as a decision model such as that shown below and the process would respond to the decision made using appropriate gateways and activities.

The business process conducts its activities to achieve one or more objectives. These are the processes goals. A process goal is started, for example, when a customer fills out an order form (Goal: Complete Customer Orders). The Goal would not be complete until the order is posted to the Enterprise Resource Planning (ERP) system or Customer Relationship Management (CRM) system. There are two types of goals that are associated with a business process: point-wise goals and steady-state goals. Point-wise goals are the goal of the process with respect to a user, customer, or stakeholder. Steady-state goals are more like continuous metric objectives: quantified and measurable.[2]

Business Process Management

Business Process Management (BPM) is the identification, understanding, and management of business processes that support an organization's business model. Ideally, these processes support a business model that adapts to changes in economics, customer preferences, and best practices. These changes might be made to the process model itself or to logic within decision models.

Business Process Modeling Patterns

Businesses generally fall into a number of categories or patterns, as do their processes. Notably, each process is different. These patterns are generalizations of common types. If a pattern that otherwise fits the scenario does not match exactly, it should not be rejected as a possible basis for modeling efforts. These patterns, plus the event and decision patterns, are described because they might match existing scenarios and offer more insight into the needed modeling. The following list is by no means exhaustive, and every process, event, or decision is different. These are just general process types. However, experience has shown that most business processes fall into one of these patterns:

> **Human-Centric:** Human-centric processes automate human activities, particularly interactions between employees, customers, managers, and other roles. Human-centric systems can include customized order-to

---

2. Martin Ould, Business Process Management: A Rigorous Approach, 2005

cash, personnel on-boarding, and complex application or claims processing.

Document Management: These processes manage documents, or more specifically, the life cycles of documents. They control versions and maintain a document repository. This often includes branches and chains of a particular document, with several levels of approvals for revisions. These processes often are found in legal systems and heavily regulated fields where there is a requirement for full auditing disclosure.

System Integrations: These processes integrate systems and applications to orchestrate their execution. The definition of the process details the validation, movement, and processing of data by different systems. Systems can run the gamut of ERP business applications, internal legacy systems, and trading partner systems.

Event-Driven: These are among the newest types of processes. The process responds appropriately to a particular event. Events are matched with processes instances that have the ability to respond to these events. Opportunities are identified through event processing: external events are evaluated, and decisions are used to identify the opportunity to which the process responds.

Examples of these processes include integrating IoT, mobile phones, advertising, and CRM systems. Based on GPS data and customer profile, a retailer can offer a nearby customer a special discount if the customer visits the store on a slow day. Smart power grids that use a process to efficiently deliver electricity to consumers is another example.

Decision-Driven: Almost every process has decisions that can be described using business logic or rules. Decision-driven processes, however, are those where a decision is central to the process. Often beginning with a decision, the flow and outcome of the process are determined as soon as the decision is made. Examples of decision driven processes include medical and insurance benefits, certain types of fraud detection, and financial or commodity applications.

Application-Centric: The application-centric process monitors integrations between various applications and controls the timing cycles and content of transferred data. This type of process monitors the input and output boundaries of applications. For example, a process can overlay the CRM, ERP, and supply chain systems. The outcome is a view that simulates a unification of these systems. This "overlay" process creates a unified view of the customer or accounting information and can settle or reduce inconsistencies regarding how data is entered and handled.

As mentioned at the start, not every process will fall into one of these patterns, and many processes have the characteristics of several. However, this list can provide a shortcut to a robust solution for business problems. Moreover, if a process needs to be deployed, these patterns will focus the technical choices that need to be made by the team.

DECISION DEFINITIONS

Business processes often need decisions to be made if they are to be completed, especially in the decision-driven pattern. In a process context, decisions are made by applying business knowledge in the form of business rules or other decision logic to process data. Such a decision may be made by a participant in the process or the business rules for the decision may be evaluated by a business rules management system that is invoked at the relevant task in the process to automate the decision-making.

From the BPM perspective, a decision is a determination about a set of business terms or concepts that selects a particular answer or value from a set of possibilities.

Decision Management

Decision management allows an organization to control, manage, and automate the repeatable decisions at the heart of its business by effectively applying business rules, analytics, and optimization technology. Focusing on decisions as a peer to business processes, Decision Management enables the development of simpler, smarter, and more agile business processes.

Business rules are central to decision management, as are business rules management systems. Decision management maximizes the ROI of business rules technology by applying it effectively. Similarly, data mining and predictive analytics provide insight for decision management. Decision management multiplies the value of analytics by focusing them on repeatable, numerous day-to-day decisions.

From the perspective of BPM, decision management is the practice of:

1. Identifying decisions within business processes—automated or manual.
2. Precisely and unambiguously representing and populating a decision model to specify how the decision should be made without adding this information to the process model itself.
3. Implementing reporting and update processes that continually refine and improve the effectiveness of decision making as well as the efficiency of the processes.

Business Decision Modeling Patterns

Like processes, decisions generally fall into a number of categories or patterns:

Eligibility or Approval—Is this customer/prospect/citizen eligible for this product/service? These decisions are policy- and regulation-heavy, and the use of a business rules management system to handle all business rules is very effective. While eligibility and approval decisions can seem fairly static, changes are often outside the control of an organization and can be imposed at short notice.

Validation—Is this claim or invoice valid for processing? The rules for validation decisions are generally fixed and repeatable. Validation is often associated with forms, and online versions of these forms are of little use without validation. The move to mobile apps makes validation even more important as end users expect near real-time approvals.

Calculation—What is the correct price/rate for this product/service? Calculations are also overwhelmingly rules-based and making them visible and manageable pays off when changes are required or when explanations must be given. Sadly, calculations are often embedded in code, making them difficult to access.

Risk—How risky is this supplier's promised delivery date, and what discount should we insist on? Making a decision that involves a risk assessment, whether it is a delivery risk or credit risk, requires balancing policies, regulation, and some formal risk assessment. The use of business analytics to make these risk assessments has largely replaced "gut checks."

Fraud— Is this claim likely to be fraudulent, and how should we process it? Fraud detection generally involves a running battle with fraudsters, offering a premium for rapid response and an ability to keep up with new types of fraud. Managing fraud decisions involves expertise and best practices as well as advanced predictive analytics.

Opportunity—What represents the best opportunity to maximize revenue? Organizations want to make sure they are making the most of every interaction, especially when dealing with customers. These decisions involve identifying the best opportunity—the one with the greatest propensity to be accepted—as well as identify when and where to promote it.

Maximizing—How can these resources be used for maximum impact? Many business decisions are made with the intention of maximizing the value of constrained resources, whether it is deciding how best to allocate credit to a card portfolio or how best to use a set of machines in a production line.

Assignment—Who should see this transaction next? A lot of business processes involve routing or assignment. Additionally, when a complex decision is automated, it is common for some percentage to be left for manual review or audit. The decisions that determine who these transactions should be routed to and how to handle delays or queuing problems can involve numerous and complex business rules.

Targeting—What exactly should we say to this person? In many situations, there is an opportunity to personalize the interaction or target someone very specifically. If businesses can combine everything known about someone with analytics that predict likely behavioral trends and best practices, and constrain this to be in compliance with privacy and other regulations, individuals can feel like the system is interacting only with them.

Business Rules and Decisions

A business rule is a statement of the action to be taken when a specific set of conditions are true. Essentially, it is an atomic logic step that uses data and knowledge to evaluate part of a proposition about a business decision. Business rules "meet" processes through decisions. Business rules decide with the information provided to the decision and when the business rules are changed, the decision outcome also is changed. A business rule is not a decision; it is a logical condition of the decision.

Business rules often evolve in a process to standardize the basis of decisions. At first, people make the decisions based on experience. With time, best practices evolve into an improved set of business rules. The rules automate the most common decisions and promote consistent results. When a decision requires a person's experience, the rule can also decide who in the organization is best qualified to make that decision.

Figure 1.2 presents a process fragment in BPMN with embedded business rules. The objective of the fragment is to assign a customer loyalty discount. The first activity computes the customer's total purchases. Next, a gateway assigns a loyalty discount. Each branch of the gateway represents a business rule.

While such a diagram is reasonably easy to read, it is clear that this approach will rapidly succumb to complexity. If discounts were calculated based on several properties of a customer, such as longevity, total purchases, and likely loyalty, then a nest of gateways and branches would be required, as shown in Figure 1.3.

A decision management approach (Figure 1.4) would identify that choosing the customer discount was a decision and would show that as an activity in the process.

A separate decision model would be used to explain how the discount was calculated in more detail. Figure 1.5 shows a simple model of this type (the elements involved in this model are described in Chapter 2).

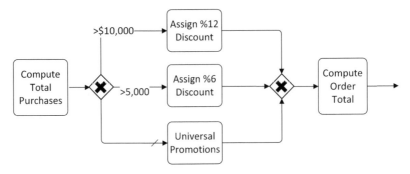

Figure 1.2 *Rules within a process model in BPMN.*

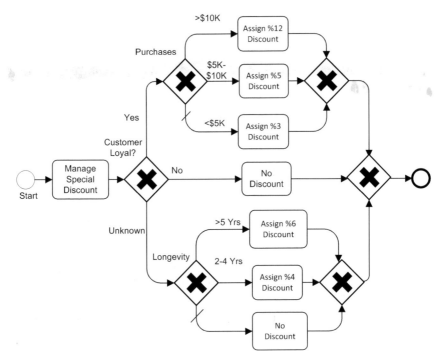

Figure 1.3 *BPMN for a complex discount decision.*

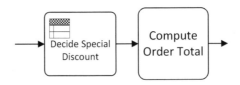

Figure 1.4 *BPMN collapsing the rules from Figure 1.2 into a decision.*

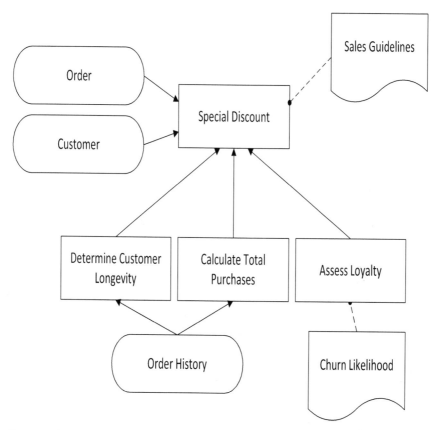

Figure 1.5 *DMN for the complex discount decision.*

Such a model makes it clear how the decision should be made, and the specific logic for the decisions in such a model can now be specified. This is often done using business rules collected into decision tables. Decisions in such a model can also rely on analytics and other algorithms instead of business rules. There are many ways to represent the decision logic involved.

Decisions and decision models provide structure for the business rules approach, allowing an enterprise's critical rules to be externalized from business processes so that they can be stored in a form that the manager and technologist understand. Analysts and subject-matter experts gather business rules to flesh out the details of a decision model.

Managing decisions and business rules empowers organizations to change business rules, and thus decision making, independently of its processes so as to adjust to its needs. Business processes are more powerful when they are designed with a decision management perspective.

BUSINESS EVENT DEFINITIONS

In a modern process modeling approach, opportunities, conditions, and factors that organizations must respond to are handled or managed with business events. Chandy and Schulte[3] define a business event as "an event that is meaningful for conducting commercial, industrial, and governmental or trade activities."

Business events are related to process modeling when the process might be involved or affected. Process modeling with BPMN includes start, intermediary, non-interrupting, and end events, which correspond directly to a process instance. Business events are not the same as BPMN events. Business events exist in a business context, such as the arrival of a purchase order or a contract default, while BPMN events are the states and transitions of a process.

Complex Event Processing (CEP) is a concept similar to business events. CEP deals with vast quantities of events that are aggregated down to a few, more significant, business events. Business events are then correlated to a business process instance or used to start a new process instance. Many business events occur outside the "bricks and mortar" of an organization. A CEP engine might detect a pattern that looks like a business event, and a decision, using business logic, will decide if the pattern is actually an event.

Business Event Management

Business event management is an emerging design technique for formalizing an enterprise's business events comprehensively and concisely. The manager and technologist catalogue the relevant events and determine how to process (e.g., filter, correlate, or archive) them. Event processing is a combination of scanning the cloud of events, applying logic to events, and transmitting the events to the appropriate channel.

Business Event Patterns

A business event has three elements: time, a combination of triggering events, and data. A business event can be explicit and simple, such as an order being placed on a website, or it can be implicit and complex, as when a customer browses 10 items from a product category while purchasing nothing. The enterprise might decide to thank the customer for shopping and offer a coupon via email. Decisions can be made to predict when the product offering is appropriate and relevant.

---

3. K. Chandy, W. Schulte, Event Processing: Designing IT Systems for Agile Companies, McGraw-Hill Osborne Media, (September 24, 2009).

Like processes and rule-supported decisions, event processing generally falls into a number of categories or patterns, as described below.

Opportunistic: A pattern of events that creates another event, which in turn starts or alters the course of a business process. For example, the pattern might be detected when activity within an online store is combined with customer profile data. The detected pattern—or new event—triggers a promotional process that offers the customer a discount. The event then triggers another decision for other offers. After a few days, the opportunity is irrelevant, and the promotional processes should terminate.

Avoidance: A pattern of events designed for risk management objectives. This pattern is commonly found in the equities and trading market where complex conditions can trigger program trading. Other events are caused by monitoring the weather and political conditions. Examples of disaster avoidance are also found in the power grid, hazardous chemical production plants, and highway traffic management.

Notifying: A pattern of events that trigger a flag or signal that will be observed by a person or a computer system. The events do not directly trigger process action. Instead, people and systems monitor event instances. An example can be found in crime prevention patterns. A criminal offender may purchase items that match the profile of prior crimes. Because this might indicate that the offender will commit a crime, the event warrants further monitoring and triggers a flag.

Notifying patterns are more data-centric than opportunistic or avoidance patterns. Data persistence (storage) is required to correlate events. In contrast, opportunistic and avoidance patterns often have significantly shorter timeframes.

Deviation: An event model that looks for variation in metrics and key performance indicators (KPIs). For example, the average number of orders per customer is 50. If a customer has more than 70 orders within a short timeframe, then a process alerts management. The customer might be added to a reseller account. Additionally, this could be a fraud indicator.

Quantitative: These patterns are the most data-intensive event patterns. A large collection of historical trending data is required to provide accurate quantitative analysis. The quantitative approach uses statistics to determine relevant events.

BUSINESS PROCESS, BUSINESS DECISIONS, AND BUSINESS EVENTS

As mentioned previously, there are three critical metaphors for business process modeling—business processes, business events, and business decisions. The table below lists the important distinctions between these three business metaphors.

Table 1.1 Characteristics of the three business process modeling metaphors

Business Event	Business Process	Business Decision
Unpredictable or random in nature (an external stimulus)	Stateful in Nature	Stateless In Nature
Monitored by the environment and filtered, sorted and correlated by rules	Sequence of activities conducted by participants	Applies business knowledge to input data
Based on observation	Sequence of activities with monitoring and control for participants	Actions, direction, control for events and processes
Improvements in observations, risk management, agility and understanding	Improvements in process metrics	More consistent policies, application of business strategy
Representation is evolving	Visual BPMN	Visual DMN

SUMMARY

The definitions and concepts covered in this chapter lays the foundation for the material in later chapters.

Over the last 10 years, process modeling in BPMN has rapidly evolved. Consistent patterns have emerged, and the use of new and powerful metaphors has become standardized. The recent addition of DMN has added maturity and depth to this important method.

The overarching objective of process modeling in BPMN and decision modeling in DMN is to understand, institutionalize, improve, and control all the components of a business model. DMN diagrams describe the operational decisions of an enterprise. BPMN/DMN diagrams accurately describe processes and connected decisions.

Many firms gather flowcharts and rules through legacy, paper-oriented procedures, or loose anecdotes of data models and "use cases." The BPMN/DMN approach is a significant improvement over these.

The core motivation of process modeling is to gather application requirements from the correct role with the correct method. The outcome is that lower-cost efforts create the process and decisions—and then get them right.

Modeling is a critical aspect of improving an existing process or business challenge. Modeling is generally done by a team of business analysts, IT personnel, and modeling experts. The outcome of the modeling is to provide a better understanding of the 'as-is' and the 'to-be'. A key aim of this book is to describe how process modeling teams illuminate verbal or tacit aspects of processes, decisions, and events with graphical notation. In addition to describing the patterns and metaphors, this book will empower readers to use these tools in process modeling activities.

CHAPTER 2

MODELING BASICS

In the introduction, BPMN concepts were defined as the key elements of a business process model. It was noted that a business process is just one of the elements in defining how an enterprise carries out its business model. However, the decision is just as critical as the process. The DMN concepts that were introduced represent the key elements for defining the decision making required by a process. This chapter presents BPMN and DMN shapes with the aim of modeling a business process, and the decisions that drive it, with the proper sequence of shapes.

In BPMN, the symbols are classified by one of four shape types: rectangle, circle, line, or diamond. The shapes define classes of behaviors that include activities, gateways, events, sequences, and flows. Markers within a shape define its behavior. All shapes reside in a participant's pool.

The four DMN symbols are represented by rectangles, ovals, documents, and clipped rectangles that represent decisions, input data, knowledge sources, and reusable business logic, respectively. These shapes have defined properties and behaviors and reside within one or more decision requirements diagrams.

At one level, a decision in DMN is modeled by arranging these shapes into a network connected by links. These links arise from their dependencies, in other words, the requirements they have for each other. With a grasp of the basic shapes and links, process modelers can easily create decision models and read DMN diagrams.

A process in BPMN is modeled by matching the use case with the proper order of shapes. Order also arises from sequences of communications. Shapes sequence with interactions or communicate with messages. With a grasp of the basic shapes and the markers, process modelers can easily create models or read BPMN diagrams.

The token passing concept is fundamental to understanding how sequences in BPMN work. It describes how the flow of a process will proceed at run time. Various BPMN elements can generate or consume tokens, and these tokens traverse a sequence flow from the start to end. Under normal conditions, a BPMN process will not be complete until all the tokens have been consumed. Later, this book will describe places, exceptions, and errors where the token can bypass the end event of the process.

It is critical to understand the preconditions for elements to execute on a BPMN model. Activities and gateways are only started when these conditions are reached. The introduction defined a business process in terms of business goals. In terms of the model, a BPMN process is a motion of data and tokens through elements and across time that follow a data-dependent course according to the values of the data. The motion of data takes place in messages, sequences, and activities.

Just as a process is modeled by parsing a use case into a sequence of BPMN shapes, a decision is modeled into a network of DMN shapes. Decision logic must sometimes be expressed very precisely and in great detail. This is especially true if an executable decision model, one whose output can provide input to the gateways and activities in BPMN, is being constructed. As a result, the DMN standard contains a lot of detail on how to specify decision logic in terms of decision tables and other elements. Very clear and detailed decision models can and should be built using only the core shapes. In general, modelers can begin by modeling decisions using the basic DMN elements and worry about the detailed decision logic language or structures later.

BPMN/DMN CONCEPTS

Over the years, there have been many evolutions of process modeling before BPMN. In the early 1900s, process modeling using flow charts was developed to represent manufacturing processes. BPMN incorporates a few concepts of flow charts and other process modeling techniques. BPMN is the settled notation; other commercial approaches include graphical editors for Business Process Execution Language (BPEL) and XML Process Definition Language (XPDL). Yet BPMN's symbols and methods are more accepted than the other techniques.

Stateless diagramming techniques like BPEL and Petri net approaches present many difficulties for business analysts.

However, it is not only its elements that make a BPMN diagram different from other modeling techniques. BPMN expresses processes in a more natural way, one that focuses on participants and controls their interactions and flow with various types of events and decisions. Because the decision is as important as the process steps, the BPM industry has created DMN. With DMN, the structure of the decision and the logic can be modeled. Decisions can be connected to a business process.

DMN has mostly evolved from the approaches taken to capture business rules. These have historically been largely focused on "verbalizing" rules or writing them out precisely and individually. However, available commercial business rules management products have long included graphical metaphors like decision graphs and decision tables to illustrate the rules. A decision model is an organizing structure for business rules, and many business rules carry out the logic of the decision. In addition, DMN models decisions can be utilized across multiple processes.

BPMN evolved from workflow modeling as provided by the familiar stencil shapes. These have historically modeled functional activities, most of which have a batch orientation, e.g., accounting processes *all* payments. BPMN uses a more process theoretic approach where participants contribute to a stream of work, e.g., accounting processes *the* payment. BPMN shapes concisely detail the essence of a business process, and DMN shapes detail the essence of the decision.

Process Instance

It is critical to understand what an instance is. The BPMN process model depicts an instance of a repeating process. Each time a process starts, an instance of the process is created or "spawned." That instance has a unique identifier and a payload of data. In many cases, the data, scope, and state of the process instance is persisted or stored. Instance persistence is critical for tracing the results of an instance.

A process can spawn or start other processes or subprocesses. These processes are connected to the master process in the scope.

Scope Context

A *scope* is a logical container or placeholder of changing information within the process instance. By default, all process instances have a hierarchy of scope context. At the top is *business process scope*, which is the high-level objective of the process. In the scope of the entire (top) process, a business objective, with well-defined start and end points, exists for the entire process. A logical division of activities and data arises as details are added to the diagram.

Data

There are a small number of shapes in BPMN for data and one in DMN, yet data is a critical part of the business process and of decisions. Nearly every shape in BPM receives input and produces output. Input data is also a critical aspect of decision modeling in DMN. The data itself is never a cause of process activity occurring. Events trigger activity, resulting in data.

The input and output of the business processes are in structured information or business objects. This might include business forms, interactions, or exchanges between computer systems, documents, activity audit logs, and data from application screens.

Each process instance holds a unique collection of data. Each process participant owns information—people provide knowledge, and systems have data. Each participant holds their own unique data state. The process maintains an abstract of the status of multiple participants, plus relevant information, in the context of a business objective. The process can contain both temporary state information (what's happening now), as well as permanent records, such as the details of a transaction.

When a process calls the logic in DMN, decisions judge or decide and direct the flow of the process. Business logic directs the decisions. The decision controls the flow and acts on the data. To reach a process decision, business rules evaluate data values. Therefore, business rules use the values from the fields in the structured process information.

Processes contribute to the data stream. Decisions also create and manipulate data. For example, a decision may decide what price to apply to an item on a requisition. This is known as a data transformation —data from the process records create other data elements. For example, an item's price might be derived from the SKU or item identifier.

In process models, message flows are used to communicate data between participants and other processes. The content of the message is process data. When this data is received by a process, a new copy exists in that process. For example, when someone sends an email, the sender has a sent item in his sent mail folder, and the recipient receives a new email item. The data contained in the message exists on both ends of the message transmission.

BASIC BPMN AND DMN SUBSET

The BPMN and DMN specifications are long, technical documents aimed at those developing software to manage process and decision models. This level of detail can seem overwhelming to those focused on *building* models, especially as there are now two canvases for modeling decisions and processes. In reality, most diagrams, whether process models or decision models, use only a subset of the shapes and other elements defined in the specifications. Knowing the basic BPMN and DMN shapes and some key concepts such as decisions, tokens, activity states, and process data is critical for effective process modeling. This chapter will concentrate on the basic shapes and concepts of BPMN 2.0 and DMN 1.0.

It is important to be able to discern between process and decision requirements. A business decision is stateless and time-invariant; when it is executable, it simply applies logic to input data. DMN is adept at documenting and implementing decisions. Moreover, business analysts can easily learn how to create and manage these decisions in DMN. These models can be extended with specific logic designed to manage complex decisions with many sub-decisions and perhaps thousands of logic steps or business rules. Processes are primarily concerned with coordinating and managing time-varying objectives and concomitant exceptions and states. BPMN is adept at managing process instances and is designed to model and document an enterprise's business process and document interactions among participants.

It is difficult to achieve computationally complex and dense logic with BPMN. BPMN lacks the compact, organizational capabilities of DMN. Similarly, DMN lacks the time-variant orchestration of activities across participants. Because the objectives are different, it is important to differentiate between processes and decision logic.

Basic BPMN Elements

Figure 2.1 lists the basic palette of BPMN that every modeler should know.

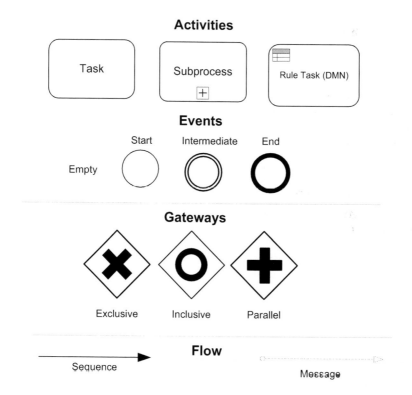

Figure 2.1   *Basic BPMN subset palette.*

Many BPMN modeling tools and BPM/workflow automation systems use only the basic BPMN subset as a menu. The full BPMN palette is quite large and requires adequate display areas. Many modeling tools offer more details and other versions of the activity, event, or gateway in a right-click or properties page for the shape. Options covered in detail in the next chapters include conditions, escalations, task types, and timing.

The subset of shapes in Figure 2.1 is sufficient for modeling basic workflow processes along a "happy path," including the connection to DMN using the rule task. The BPMN specification builds upon these basic shapes. It is critical to understand how the basic subset works across a flow before moving into more complex shapes. Later chapters of this book will describe how and why to use more complex shapes. Many of these shapes are driven by the need to handle errors and exceptions, and the basic flow of concepts is similar.

Basic DMN Elements

The core of the DMN standard is relatively straightforward, using only four shapes and three links. These shapes and links are shown in Figure 2.2.

This shapes palette allows users to develop a wide variety of decision models from very high-level summaries of manual decision making to detailed representations of the logic for an automated system. After describing BPMN shapes, the DMN shape types and requirement links will be defined.

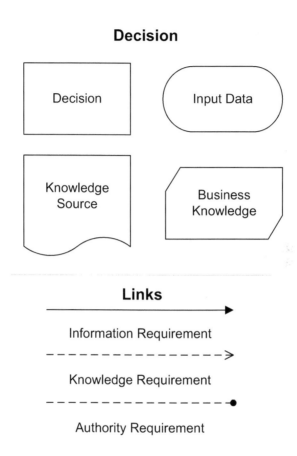

Decision

Decision

Input Data

Knowledge
Source

Business
Knowledge

Links

Information Requirement

Knowledge Requirement

Authority Requirement

Figure 2.2 *Basic DMN palette.*

BPMN BASIC DETAILS

Activity

An *activity* is work the participant performs in business processes. Activities are the basic units of process work. In its simplest form, the activity can be atomic (lowest level, indivisible unit of work) or non-atomic (involving many steps). Processes and subprocesses are compound activities. In BPMN, the types of process activities include tasks and subprocesses.

Activity shapes include four basic types:

Task A rounded rectangle showing the finest, or atomic, process step. It cannot be broken down to a finer level.	
Subprocess (collapsed) A rounded rectangle that can contain a series of other steps. The other steps are hidden from view; the plus sign indicates additional information.	
Subprocess (expanded) A rounded rectangle showing all the subprocess activities (from the collapsed subprocess).	
Rule Task A rounded rectangle denoting a connection to a decision modeled in DMN[a].	

a. Business Rules Tasks were originally envisioned as a way to link BPMN models to business rule execution directly, but the advent of the DMN standard means that, in general, these tasks should link to decision models instead.

The task is the atomic activity. Because it is atomic, there are no further details. The subprocess is a compound activity that might contain other activities. An activity can be manual, as when a human participant completes the activity, or it might be automated by a system participant.

As defined, the activity is a core part of the business process.

Examples of activities include:

- Inspecting material delivery
- Restoring a server
- Completing contract requisitions

- Deciding to approve a requisition
- Reviewing loan applications

An activity defines where a process step occurs and is a discrete unit of work. This can range from an atomic step, such as a form for entering a record, to an entire system's work, such as contract management or system maintenance.

By specification, all activities have input and output data. In some cases, input data must be ready for the activity to take place. The input and output variables in BPMN are merely placeholders for business objects that would be contained within the process. For example, a user might create a requisition data type that becomes a document attached to the input and output types. The effect of the activity might be to change data elements on the document and pass the output data down to other gateways and activities to process.

A subprocess encloses a set of BPMN elements. Essentially, any processes can be enclosed in a subprocess. Additionally, the system running the subprocess will create a thread and assign separate resources to the subprocess. When the subprocesses are done executing, they return to the process that contains them.

The business rule task shape denotes the place within the process model that calls up a DMN model and obtains the decision output. For the purposes of this text, the rule shape denotes a connection to DMN. The inputs of a rule task are processed by the logic defined in the DMN model and then output for use in downstream gateways and activities. Decisions can affect or control a process in specific ways. Later chapters in this book will explore this control in detail.

Process Flow

Flow is the order (and data) in which the activities or process steps are performed, and it has a time dimension. As time advances, the process proceeds along its flow. Multiple flows might occur within multiple participant roles. Importantly, the correct BPMN shape defines how flows can be sequenced. Sequences might run in order or in parallel. There are two types of flows in a BPMN diagram:

- **Sequence**—Defines the order in which activities are performed for any given process participant. Sequence flow never occurs between participants.
- **Message**—Defines the flow of information and messages between participants within a process. Messages never occur within the same participant.

Sequence

Sequence lines are denoted by a solid line ending with an arrowhead. The arrow shows the flow or sequence of a process. This is frequently called *sequence flow*.

The sequence that is activated can also be considered the traversal of a single token. This is denoted[1]:

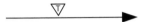

Tokens will not be shown in every diagram in this book; however, it can be inferred that every active sequence is associated with a conceptual token. Sequence lines define the sequence flow or transition between the logical steps performed by a participant. In Figure 2.3 below, for example, the contract is awarded after the bids are evaluated (both by the contract office). Bid Evaluation transitions to Contract Award within the contract office.

The sequence is a transition within the hand-off between activities. A transition is more than a connection from one process step to the next. Transition means that one activity has stopped and another has started. A transition sequence might simultaneously split into many paths.

A transition is conceptualized through the sequence flow line. A sequence flow from one activity or event to the next shows the next as starting—or enabled to start. In the example, Bid Evaluation is complete, and Contract Award is started.

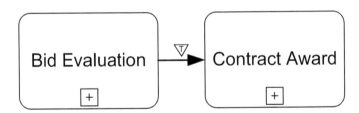

Figure 2.3 *Sequence flow.*

---

1. The T within an inverted triangle is the suggested notation within the OMG specification. Tokens are shown to explain the execution semantics of the diagram.

The token is a mental kluge for understanding how BPMN models proceed. On the timeline of a process, there are three phases of activity: before, during, and after. As shown in Figure 2.4, the basic states are:

Ready: Pre-execution, an activity is ready for execution if the required number of tokens has arrived—if multiple tasks might need to be completed.

Active: During execution, the required input data is available and the activity is performing work or waiting for completion.

Completed: All the prerequisites are done, and a token is generated for the next sequence.

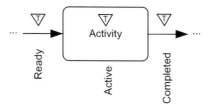

Figure 2.4 *This illustrates the timeline of an activity. More states will be described in later chapters.*

What happens if there is an error? There are other states that a task can encounter, e.g., business exceptions and system errors. These will be detailed in later chapters. The basic phases of an activity are in these three steps. Moreover, it does not matter what type of activity is in the processes, as all activities, gateways, and events cycle through these steps.

As a minimum, a single sequence and token is always generated for a completed activity.

Message Flows

Messaging is a prominent feature of BPMN. *Messages* are the mechanism for processes to communicate. Participants are triggered to act as a result of messages, which can start an instance of a process. Process modelers use messages to queue work assignments, control running processes, and communicate with customers and partners.

Messages are represented with a dashed line, with a circle at the starting end and an arrowhead on the other end. The arrow shows the *message flow* direction.

Messages never occur from one shape to another within the same process. Messages only occur between participants and processes. Unlike sequence flow, there is no token associated with a message flow.

The token concept is designed to model parallelism and deadlocking within a process. However, if a task or event shows an incoming message, then the token will wait for the message to arrive at the starting boundary. Nothing else will occur in this branch of the process until the message arrives.

Interactions are important aspect of process modeling, and BPMN interactions are represented by the message flow. Participants interact with each other using a message flow. For instance, the "Contracting Officer" awards the winning bid to the "Contractor." The message is in the award. By definition, participants use messages to interact.

Fingar and Smith[1] mention that an interaction is the use of process desktops that allow people or participants to interact with the process. This includes workflow that emphasizes assignment, task management, and form-based data entry. Interactions gave rise to the idea of task-oriented process instances that are started by a form. This is common in existing process monitor and task lists in BPM suites. A form activity is a complete interaction that is spawned from interaction with a process instance.

PROCESS FLOW WITH GATEWAYS, SPLITS, AND MERGES

Processes can take multiple paths, and models depict various sequences of activities. A flow can split directly from the activity into parallel branches, or gateways can provide explicit control.

A *gateway* splits and merges paths in a BPMN diagram at a point. A gateway also generates or consumes tokens at a specific point in a BPMN diagram. Gateways direct sequence flows with data or specify various path splits. The simple gateway shape is an empty diamond, as shown below.

---

1. Howard Smith and Peter Fingar: Business Process Management: The Third Wave." (Meghan Kiffer Pr, October 2002).

By default, the simple gateway shape specifies a behavior: data-based exclusive gateway. The exclusive gateway is denoted with an X marker inside the diamond. For the rest of this book, more descriptive gateway shapes will be used.

While it may appear that a difference exists between a splitting gateway and a merging gateway, as if there are two types of gateways, the reality is that the gateways always act in a bidirectional manner. They simultaneously merge and split. Like the activity, there are specific conditions which activate a gateway for splitting. In general, paths start with a single, incoming sequence into a gateway; however, there are occasionally reasons to merge and split in the same gateway. To learn the nature of gateways, process modelers must learn both the rule for splitting and merging. That means learning which sequences (therefore tokens) are activated and which are consumed on the merge. Like the activity, gateways also change states, particularity when waiting for the proper number of tokens to arrive.

Implicit Splits and Merge

It is not necessary to use a gateway to split a process flow into a parallel path of merge pates. In a simple merge, flow paths and the resulting tokens are rejoined at an activity. Consider a product moving through an inspection process in an inventory process. If there is no defect, the modeler notes that the following activity is Mark Passed. The "If … Then" dialog suggest we need choice of paths. Otherwise, the defect is identified and reported. In Figure 2.5, the paths that split after Inspect Item are rejoined (merged) at Shelf Item.

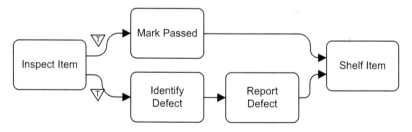

Figure 2.5 *Implicit merge in an inventory process.*

This is called an implicit merge because the merge is implied—the tasks merge, rejoining at Shelf Item with undefined conditions. The diagram fragment in Figure 2.5 does not specify how the Mark Passed task and Report Defect merge. The diagram's intentions might initially seem obvious; however, the design can be deceptive.

Implicit merges appear ambiguous. However, the specification document precisely defines how they should be executed. The process will not wait until both Mark Passed and Report Defect tasks complete before continuing to Shelf

Item; it will pass the token to the Shelf Item. For these reasons, and because there is no flow control, the Shelf Item task might be executed more than once, which is probably not the process modeler's intention.

The recommendation is to explicitly specify the transition from Inspect Item to Identify Defect with gateways or flow controls. This avoids having to remember the behavior for the implicit process merge. Otherwise, the process diagram should describe the merge behavior at the Shelf Item point with more shapes. Figure 2.6 shows an exclusive choice in defining conditions for the two paths leaving the Inspect Item task.

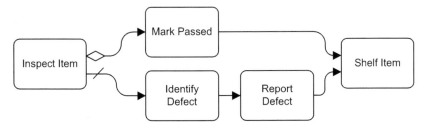

Figure 2.6 *Splitting paths with a condition.*

The diamond symbol on a sequence shows the process path when data matches a specified transition condition. The sequence flow line with the slash marks a default path. A condition is a Boolean expression based on process data that control a sequence of activities. This data is often the input or output of an activity. For instance, a condition might assess the value of a Pass Inspection flag and follow the transition to Marked Passed when the value is YES. The Pass Inspection flag is the output of an activity. The process follows the default path when the transition condition fails to be true. Whenever conditional paths are specified, use a default path.

Figure 2.6 shows how the process takes a path to eitherMark Passed orIdentify Defect. A default path clearly states that either path can occur, but not both. By definition, the default path has no condition. The default path indicates the sequence flow that is taken when all other paths do not meet their prescribed conditions. Only one token would pass along these sequences, so the Shelf Item task would be executed once.

Data-Based Exclusive Gateways

The data-based exclusive gateway is a diamond shape with an enclosed X, as shown here.

The data-based gateway shapes are either *exclusive* or *inclusive*. The term *data-based* means the data in the process, often the input or output of activities, selects which transition to take based on a condition in the data. In the data-based exclusive gateway, process data defines conditions for the paths leaving the gateway.

In the exclusive gateway, the shape is activated when a single token arrives. If multiple merging sequences are input to the exclusive gateway, each token that arrives activates the shape. The gateway then evaluates a condition and decides which path to execute. The exclusive gateway should therefore be used when the process moves exclusively along only one path. For example, examine Figure 2.7.

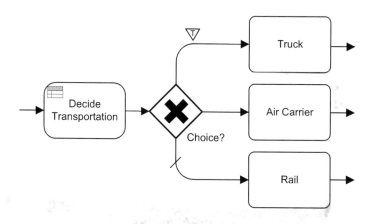

Figure 2.7   *Data-based, exclusive gateways. Only one token will leave the gateway, which in this case is the truck.*

The activity Decide Transportation in Figure 2.7 is drawn as a business rule task. This marks a place in the process where a decision, modeled in DMN, can be called. The gateway needs data to evaluate a gateway expression, which in this case is the expression evaluated to Truck. Logic in the decision model evaluates the provided data and decides the mode of shipment. This is the principal mechanism for an operational decision to affect process flow.

The Truck, Air Carrier, and Rail tasks appear after deciding what form of transportation will be used. The gateway specifies exclusive behavior; the flow takes only one path and spawns one token; and all others are excluded. The sequence flow line to the Rail has a marker indicating the default path. In this example, the designer has chosen Rail as the default. It is necessary to use a default path whenever conditional flows exist.

The exclusive gateway merges paths by waiting for the first token to arrive so the use of the gateway is optional for exclusive paths. Figure 2.8 depicts a fragment of a supply chain process.

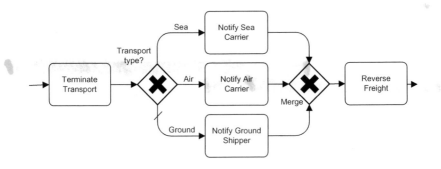

Figure 2.8 *An explicit merge for the exclusive data-based gateway with a default condition.*

Since one token emerges from the gateway after the Terminate Transport task, the lines can be connected from the notification tasks directly to the Reverse Freight task. The exclusive data path specifies the merge point, at which the final Reverse Freight task is run.

For diagram and process clarity, an explicit merge gateway is recommended. In most cases, it is good standard practice to use an exclusive gateway shape for a merge point if the branch starts with an exclusive gateway. In Figure 2.8, the exclusive gateways for both split and merge document appear the end of the three paths. As a diagram becomes more detailed, dozens of steps might be taken between Terminate Transport and Reverse Freight. This might be especially true if a process diagram spans several pages. With merge shapes at the end of paths, the diagram becomes much easier to read. Since parallel and inclusive gateway shapes need a shape to merge flows, the exclusive merge gateway shape is consistent with the rest of the diagram.

As mentioned, BPMN includes a data-based inclusive gateway. Therefore, it might seem logical to describe this gateway next. However, an understanding of the concept of parallelism in processes is needed first.

Parallel Gateways

A *parallel gateway* is a diamond shape with an enclosed cross, as shown below.

In the parallel gateway, the shape is activated when all the tokens on the active, upstream sequences arrive. If multiple merging sequences are input to the parallel gateway, then each token must arrive to activate the shape. So the parallel gateway should be used when the process moves in parallel across two or more paths.

In the parallel gateway, all paths leaving the gateway are executed (Figure 2.9), and a token is generated for each path. This gateway is used in places where the process unconditionally follows multiple branches. In other words, after the parallel gateway, all the activities occur simultaneously. Parallelism is best when sequential execution is not efficient—for instance, when one long-running activity might delay other activities. Here the parallel gateway shape is used to show multiple activities being performed simultaneously.

For each path, a new, concurrent thread is spawned on the parallel branches, and each path receives a token. This means that each path is assigned separate computing resources.

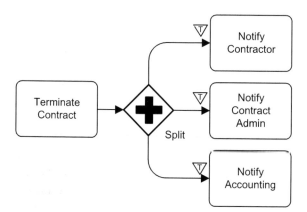

Figure 2.9 *In a parallel gateway, all paths will be taken simultaneously, and tokens are generated for each path.*

There is no default condition for the parallel gateway. All paths are unconditionally taken, and the transition to all paths occurs simultaneously.

When deciding whether or not to use a parallel gateway, there are several
things to consider:

- Are all tasks always executed? If not, use an exclusive or inclusive data-
  based gateway.
- Are there any dependent tasks? When there is a dependency, use a
  sequence of tasks rather than parallel.
- What is the impact on the subsequent tasks if all paths occur
  simultaneously?
- In later activities, should the process continue sequentially rather than in
  parallel?
- This determines where the parallel sequence flows need to merge before
  subsequent tasks can begin.

Most often, parallelism is needed for organizational reasons, as when several
groups work on parallel tasks, or for efficiency where time- or resource-intensive
tasks can be run in parallel. For example, external activities such as lab testing or
external reviews might take place in parallel, while internal administrative tasks
continue.

An explicit gateway merge uses a gateway shape to show multiple paths combining. For the process to move beyond the merging gateway, all tokens must
arrive at the merge where they are consumed.

Figure 2.10 shows implicitly merging paths after a gateway shape.

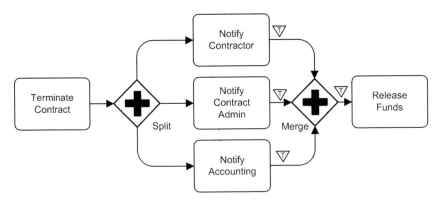

Figure 2.10 *An improper implicit merge with a parallel split.*

Exactly what happens at the merge point—the Release Funds task? The parallel gateway following the Terminate Contract task says that notification of the

contractor, contractor administrator, and accounting occurs in parallel. Each begins or enters the active state at the same time. Each has a separate token. The notification tasks require different times to complete. One may conclude before the other sends the token to the next activity for execution. An implicit merge acts like an exclusive merge so the release funds might be executed three times in this figure. The diagram does not provide the solution desired. Here is an example of why:

If the Release Funds task should not occur three times, then the process might be clearer with a parallel merge. The parallel merge shape is identical to the parallel split. Placement is the only difference between the parallel split and merge.

In an explicit parallel merge, progress does not move beyond the gateway until all the incoming tokens have arrived. In our earlier discussion, a token is not created on the outgoing paths of the activity until the activity has completed. Thus, the outgoing tokens from the three parallel activities signal the completion of their task.

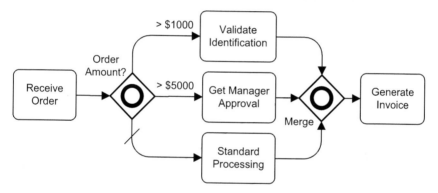

Figure 2.11 *Proper merging of parallel paths. The three tokens on the parallel tasks are consumed by the merging gate, and one is produced.*

At the diagram's merge point, before the Release Funds task, all paths must complete before continuing. The Release Funds task is dependent on the completion of the three notifications; the process will coordinate all paths.

Data-Based Inclusive Gateway

The *data-based inclusive gateway* is a diamond shape with an enclosed circle, as shown here:

In a splitting path, multiple paths could conditionally be taken, and this gateway is called inclusive. The gateway evaluates process data against a condition, which is where the term *data-based* originates. The gateway generates tokens for all sequence flows that have a condition that evaluates to True.

The inclusive gateway shape is a hybrid of the data-based exclusive and parallel gateways. There is a condition for each flow path, and one or more of the conditional paths might be taken. A thread is spawned for each path taken, and separate computing resources are assigned.

Figure 2.12 presents a fragment of an order management process. Depending on the order total, various processing steps must be taken.

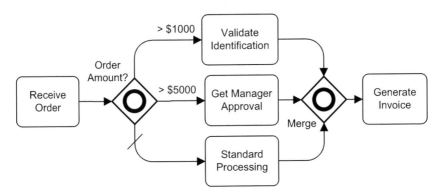

Figure 2.12 *An explicit merge with a data-based inclusive gateway.*

After the Receive Order task executes, the other paths execute whenever associated conditions are true. If the order amount is over $1000, then additional validation occurs to prevent fraud. Additionally, orders over $5000 must be approved by a manager. When none of the conditional paths are taken, the process takes the default path. If the order total is not over $1000, only the standard processing activity occurs.

Default conditions should be defined for inclusive gateways. A deadlock occurs if no default path is specified, and no condition evaluates to true. The parallel gateway passes one incoming token. In a deadlock, the process cannot go past the gateway, and the token will not pass. It never continues or completes, and the token has nowhere to go.

Merging the inclusive gateway: When it is time for the inclusive gateway to merge, the gateway waits for all incoming tokens to arrive. Again, use of explicit merging for parallel sequences is a best practice.

As shown in Figure 2.13, there are alternate constructions for inclusive gateways. The activities can be split into a number of exclusive branches. Using exclusive branches may mean bypassing activities under other conditions.

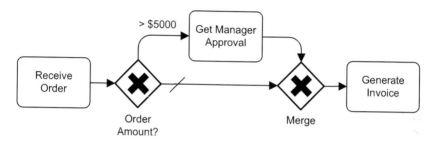

Figure 2.13 *A data-based exclusive gateway controlling an optional step.*

In Figure 2.13, the Receive Order process takes the extra step (Get Manager Approval) when the order amount is more than $5,000. By default, the Get Manager Approval activity is bypassed. With this notation, it is simple to create a default path to bypass the extra step.

Inclusive gateways might also use transitions without activities. In Figure 2.14, the process's default path bypasses all the conditional paths. Without one or more conditions in the gateway evaluating to True, the process takes the default path—straight to the merge point—with no additional activities.

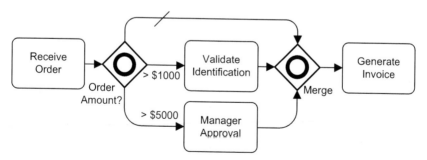

Figure 2.14 *Inclusive gateway with a default bypass path.*

Figure 2.14 shows an order management process fragment. The Standard Processing task in Figure 2.14 was replaced with a default path void of activity. As an inclusive gateway, the default path is not taken if any conditional path is true. One or more other tasks (e.g. Validate Identification, Manager Approval) can occur in parallel.

Gateway Labels

The transitions entering the gateway in Figures 2.10 through 2.14 are labeled. Document gateway works with labels in a question format. For instance, a clear label might be "Selected color?" The sequence flow transitions leaving the gateway should be labeled to answer the question the gateway asks. Red, blue, and green could be possible answers to the question. In Figure 2.15, the answers to the question "Order Amount?" are covered by the conditions >$1,000 and >$5,000.

Gateways often follow tasks that involve decision making. These tasks decide the appropriate value, and the gateway then directs the process to follow a path appropriate to the value. Modeling the decision making for such a task separately as a decision model allows for a sophisticated process while keeping complexity out of the process model.

Inclusive/Exclusive Gateway Best Practices

There are a few best practices that should be considered with inclusive and exclusive gateways:

- Limit use of the inclusive gateway to situations needing parallel execution. In other situations, try to use multiple exclusive gateways. This reduces assigning unnecessary computing resources.
- Avoid using the inclusive gateway for multiple unrelated conditions. A gateway should ask only one question—for example, Selected Color, Low Inventory, and Order Amount More Than $5,000 should be assigned to separate exclusive gateways.
- If multiple gateways are used repeatedly, then consider that these gateways represent a decision that can be modeled in a decision model and assigned to a new task followed by a single gateway.

AD HOC SUBPROCESS

In some circumstances, we do not know the order in which the activities in a subprocess will be completed. Perhaps there are a number of independent, external information items that are arriving randomly. Another analogy is shopping for items against a list when one does not know where the items will be located. For this pattern, BPMN has provided the *ad hoc subprocess*.

Not all the activities within an ad hoc subprocess are connected by sequences. Upon execution, all activities that have no incoming sequence are enabled. If the subprocess is sequential, the activities within are selected one by one, usually with human intervention. If they are parallel, all enabled activities are selected for execution.

Figure 2.15 depicts a vendor evaluation process from a Supplier Relations Management (SRM) process. The four activities must be completed, yet there is no apparent order to the evaluation steps.

As shown in Figure 2.15, a tilde marker is shown on the subprocess shape when it is ad hoc.

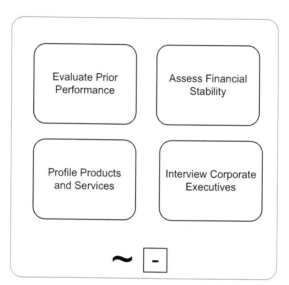

Figure 2.15 *Example of an ad hoc process.*

Activities inside any subprocess start with the first shape in a sequence flow. All activities must transition to the completed state before the subprocess is complete. Therefore, subprocesses also include an implicit merge.

The ad hoc subprocess simplifies some complex patterns. During the development of a diagram, when the execution order is yet unknown, the ad hoc subprocess is used. A parallel split or a defined sequence flow with gateways describes most processes. In the shopping cart example, however, the ad hoc subprocess shows the desired pattern with the minimum of shapes.

PROCESS EVENT

An *event* is something that happens. A *business event* is something that happens that is relevant to the organization. The business event is often external to the organization and random. A *process event* defines a point where the process is either started, stopped, halted, or continued. Events might direct a process from the original flow into an alternate path. Importantly, events define occurring activities of interest. Normally, participant actions, choices, or activities define or create events. An empty event has undefined criteria, whereas other BPMN event types have a specific trigger condition.

All event shapes are circular, as in the empty start shape below.

The event shape defines various points within the progress, ending, or exceptions of the process. It can be at the start of a process, the end of a process, or within a process flow.

Empty Events

An *empty event* is a simple event that denotes a start, stop, or intermediate point in the process. The event shape is further divided into three major categories, as shown here:

Start Event This is used at the start of a process. Start event shapes are drawn as a single thin line circle. They produce one token.	
Intermediate Event This is used between the start and the end of a process. Intermediate event shapes are drawn as a <u>double thin line</u> circle. The token is passed.	
End Event This is used to show where a process flow may end. The shape is drawn with a <u>thick solid line</u>. The end consumes one token.	

The BPMN specification allows a process to start with either a task or a gateway. Unless there are multiple events that start a process, a single, empty start event is a better choice for starting a process diagram. Start events explicitly show how and where the process starts. Here, it starts with a single token.

Examples of events include:

- Contract order submitted
- Database unavailable
- Contract requisition completed
- Requisition rejected
- Loan application received

There are various types of events that model these examples. Consider the diagram in Figure 2.16 without the start and end events. With or without the start and end events, the process in the diagram is the same. The events denote the start and end points for the reader.

The simple process starts with one start event and one token. The end event, however, may be used more than once in a pool; they must consume every token. Figure 2.16 shows the usage of more than one end event.

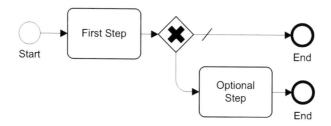

Figure 2.16a   *Ending examples using a gateway.*

Adding the gateway after the First Step task, the optional path is the Optional Step task. Under certain conditions, the process ends. A process end is an event, not a task. Adding the end event simplifies the diagram. Without the end event after the Optional Step task, there would be an implicit end. Explicit shapes refine a process design's clarity. In terms of the tokens, the exclusive gateway passes one token to one of the sequences. The end event consumes the token, and the process can end properly.

The intermediate empty shape, the double circle, specifies a point of interest in the diagram or shows a place where the state or status changes. Since the shape is an empty event, and behavior is not specified, the description for this shape is uncertain. Consider a business process that has entered a new status. For example, it might transition from Pending to Approved.

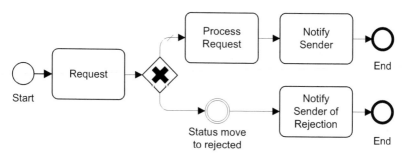

Figure 2.16b   *Examples of intermediate events in a process.*

The intermediate empty event documents a point, such as a Key Performance Indicator (KPI), in the diagram. KPIs quantify objectives that measure the strategic performance of an organization. When a status changes to rejected in the process example, a KPI might be the number of rejected requests. In addition to recording status counts, the process might record more process data at this point. To track this data, a business builds Business Intelligence (BI) and Business Activity Monitoring (BAM) into the processes.

The rules for the proper use of the intermediate empty event are:

1. A transition line must leave and enter an intermediate shape[1]; otherwise, use a start or end event.

2. The intermediate empty event does not show any delay in the process.

3. The intermediate empty event does not have any conditions associated with it.

4. The intermediate empty event does not imply a point of synchronization.

Terminate Event

The *terminate event* causes all activities in a process to be immediately ended, and its shape in a BPMN diagram is depicted below:

The terminate event shape can be used to cancel all activities in a process. All the tokens will be consumed.

In Figure 2.17, the activities Search for Candidates and Negotiate Contract are enabled to occur in parallel. If contract negotiation fails, it is useless to look for project staff. If the gateway Continue condition is No, then the process will terminate. This includes all activity and the related tokens in the Search for Candidates subprocess. Since the Search for Candidates subprocess is ongoing and does not merge with the parallel flow, a terminate event is an excellent option to stop both flows and consume all the tokens.

A terminate event is not used for a process flow that stops normally; rather, it is used for abnormal circumstances. Unless there is a specific intention to terminate, an end event such as in the example above should be used.

---

1. An exception to the rule is when an intermediate shape is used on a subprocess boundary. Another exception is where the event-based subprocess is used. These will be discussed later.

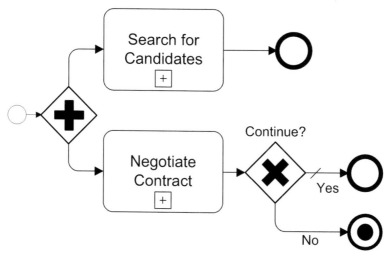

Figure 2.17 *Usage of the terminate event.*

PARTICIPANT POOL

Designers of the BPMN notation have founded the process on the basis of the participant. A *participant* is an actor or a person that interacts in a process. The actor includes any human, digital, or virtual resource that is involved in a business process. Participants can include people, systems, machines, other processes, groups of people, and groups of systems.

The pool shape represents the participant and contains the elements of a process flow performed by the process participant.

Figure 2.18 *Pool.*

The pool creates a context for the diagram, referring to a participant. Participants can be specified, such as a manager in HR, or they can be a type of role or organization.

Processes can also be participants. From a modeling perspective, a process is treated just like another participant. Sometimes processes interact with each other.

Contract receipting is a good example: The Inventory Receipt process hands off to inspectors. This starts the Inventory Inspection process, which hands off to material receipting, which then starts the Invoicing process. These hand offs conclude with the Accounts Payable process.

Examples of People participants include:

- Inventory receipt clerk inspecting the order.
- Customer Service Rep answering a request.
- Employee filling out a requisition.
- Patient in a hospital.
- Manager approving a requisition.
- Technician restoring a disk drive.
- A loan officer reviewing an application.

System Participants:

- Oracle Financials, JD Edwards, SAP, PeopleSoft.
- Database server.
- Business Rules Management System.
- A telephony queuing switch.
- A web service.
- An application server, e.g., Enterprise JavaBeans (EJB) or method.
- A custom-built User Interface (UI).
- An enterprise service business or message broker (Sonic, MQ-Series, or Tuxedo queue).

Participants might also be roles. A *role* is a logical grouping of people and systems that perform a general work category in the process diagram's context. People and systems can have different roles, and roles rarely mix people and systems. For example, a person enters data, and a system receives and processes the data. Although people and systems perform similar work, the role recognizes a division of responsibility within a business process.

BPMN allows for a further breakout of pools into logical groupings called *lanes*. In some cases, this could suggest a role for the participant, such as legal, recruiting, or contract negotiation. A pool itself is one participant. In BPMN, the role is defined on the pool, and the lane is used to group activity. For example, Figure 2.19 shows the contracting office (a role), with activity groupings in lanes (Contract Negotiation and Staffing Search).

Using lanes is optional. The addition of lanes often adds clarity to the diagram.

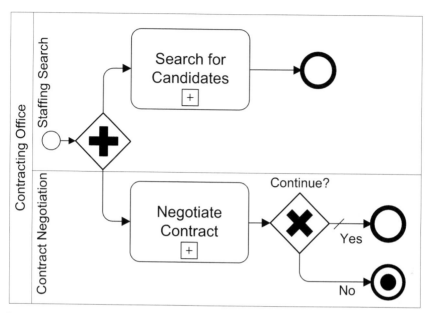

Figure 2.19 *Addition of pool and lanes to the project ramp-up process.*

To clarify the application of lanes, consider that all activity within a pool is being performed by one participant. The parallel shape indicates that this participant is potentially conducting multiple activities simultaneously. If the process modeler wants to show that more than one participant is involved, another pool is used. Messaging (covered in the next chapter) is used to coordinate activity between participants.

Another common style of BPMN is to show several roles, such as HR, accounting, sales, and legal, all in one pool and divided by lanes. A pool represents a single participant, which can be people, systems, or processes. When the pool represents a process, the roles in that process could logically be grouped into lanes. This is a common approach used in many popular BPM/Workflow Automation systems.

DMN BASIC DETAILS

This section presents DMN shapes with the aim of modeling a business decision with the proper arrangement of shapes.

Decision

```
┌────────────────────────────────────┐
│                                     │
│              Decision               │
│                                     │
└────────────────────────────────────┘
```

A *decision* is represented by a rectangle that contains at least its name. A decision determines an output from a number of inputs by applying some decision logic. As was discussed earlier, decisions can be decomposed into sub-decisions. Top level decisions can be thought of as selecting an action from a range of possible actions. Lower level decisions often will simply provide input to other decisions. All decisions, at whatever level of granularity, are represented the same way, and there are no subtypes.

Decisions have a number of properties that may be recorded as part of documenting requirements (see Chapter 3), but two properties should be captured for every decision as soon as possible:

- **Question:** A natural language statement that represents the decision in the form of a question. This should be specific and detailed.

- **Allowed Answers:** A natural language description of the possible answers to this question. If the decision is an action-oriented one, this will describe the possible actions that could be taken. Otherwise, it will be a description of the form of the information determined by the decision.

For action-oriented decisions, the allowed answers represent the responses that the process must handle when the decision model is invoked by a business rules task as noted above.

DMN allows these properties to be displayed with the decision node, but because this tends to make diagrams cluttered, a succinct name is preferred.

Input Data

```
 ╭──────────────────────────────────────╮
(                                          )
(              Input Data                  )
(                                          )
 ╰──────────────────────────────────────╯
```

Input data is represented by an oval that contains, at the very least, its name. Decisions require inputs, and many of these are input data, which is data that is input to the decision making from outside the decision context. When a decision is modeled and linked to an activity, input data is the data that can be passed to the decision from the process.

Input data elements typically represent business entities that are being used in the decision making, such as Policy or Customer. However, sometimes they can represent any information element at any level of detail. Each input data element can be described in terms of a hierarchical information model that specifies exactly what information elements comprise the input data. This detailed information is linked to the input data element but not displayed.

Knowledge Source

Knowledge sources are represented by a document shape that contains, at the very least, its name. Knowledge sources represent the source of know-how for making a decision. This could be regulations or policies about how a decision must be made, best practices or expertise about how it should be made, or even analytic knowledge about how it might be made more accurately. Knowledge sources are the authorities for a decision and typically refer to some external document or source that contains detailed guidance.

Business Knowledge Model

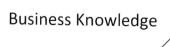

Business knowledge models are represented by a rectangle with clipped corners. Business knowledge models represent functions that encapsulate reusable decision making logic. The logic they encapsulate might be a set of business rules, a decision tree, a decision table, or an analytic model. The specifics of knowledge representation involved need not be displayed on the diagram but could be.. The initial DMN specification does not provide any notation for this, however.

The decision logic that can be specified in a business knowledge model can also be linked directly to a decision. They are equivalent in their ability to contain detailed decision logic, but encapsulating it in a business knowledge model allows it to be reused, parameterized and displayed on a Decision Requirements Diagram.

DECISION REQUIREMENTS

The four shapes—decisions, input data, knowledge sources, and business knowledge models—comprise the nodes in all decision requirements diagrams. The links between these nodes are requirements links, denoting one of three kinds of requirements.

Information Requirements

The primary requirement link, shown by a solid arrow, is an *information requirement*. These are used to show the inputs to a decision. If a decision requires a piece of information, then it will have an appropriate information requirement link. The element at the blunt end of the link is required by the decision at the arrow end.

Two elements can participate as the source of an information requirement: decisions and input data.

- Where a decision requires information from outside the decision making context, it will have an input requirement to an input data element that represents that information.

- Where a decision requires information produced by making another decision that will be shown by an information requirement, that links the precursor decision to the decision.

DMN does not provide a notation to show if an information requirement is mandatory or optional. For example, a marketing decision that requires both the result of a decision to see if an anonymous customer can be identified and information about the customer. Each of these would have different requirements for the results. Obviously the information about the customer is only required if the result of the decision is a successful customer identification. This means that the customer information is not required every time the decision is made. This is useful to know and to document in the decision's description, but it is not shown with the notation.

Information requirements to input data can also be shown using the listed data option, which lists the names of the input data elements in the lower half of a decision element, separate from the name of the decision, using a horizontal line.

Listing input data this way is the equivalent of linking the decision to the input data using information requirements links.

Decision
Input Data 1 Input Data 2

Authority Requirements

Authority requirements show where the process needs to go to find out how to make a decision. Shown by a dashed line with a round end, authority requirements identify that the element at the blunt end is an authority for the element at the round end. This allows for a knowledge source to be linked to a decision to show that it contains some of the knowledge needed to make that decision.

Authority requirements are purely documentary and have no impact on execution.

Knowledge Requirements

If business knowledge models are being used, then *knowledge requirements* show how those business knowledge models are invoked to make decisions. The business knowledge model at the blunt end is used by the decision or business knowledge model at the arrow end.

DECISION REQUIREMENT DIAGRAMS

These four elements—decisions, input data, knowledge sources, and business knowledge models—can be combined to create decision requirement diagrams. The relationships created by adding requirements links to these diagrams produce a network of linked elements and form the basis of a decision model.

Multiple decision requirements diagrams can be developed, and the model contains all the relationships specified on any diagram. There is no need for any particular diagram to be complete, and no one diagram needs to show all the requirement's relationships in which a given element participates. Experience so far suggests that there are numerous ways to use the diagrams.

Decision Context

When a decision is first identified, it is generally useful to document the obvious input data and knowledge sources for that decision. These decisions will generally be those that are at the top of the decomposition, meaning no other decisions are dependent on them. These decisions do not participate as the source of any information requirement associations. These decisions will often be executed directly by a business rules task in a business process.

The data objects available in the business process at the point of decision are likely to be the basis for the input data for the decision, though there may be others, and not all the available information may be needed by the decision. An initial set of knowledge sources can be determined using standard analysis and elicitation techniques.

Figure 2.21 presents a decision requirement diagram for the transportation example. The information requirements include the capabilities of a facility receiving a shipment and the agreements with carriers to move products. Facilities are limited by the modes of shipments that they can receive and the rate at which the material can be moved into inventory. There are also certain regulatory restrictions on the movement of materials.

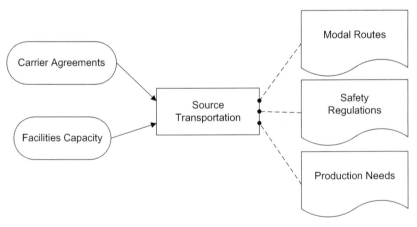

Figure 2.20 *A decision requirements diagram showing decision context.*

Initial Decomposition

The second common use of a decision requirements diagram is to break down a decision into its components to illustrate the decision in more detail. This involves identifying the decisions that must be made before the overall decision can be made, which are the decisions whose output it requires, and linking tho-seusing information requirements. If some of the newly identified decisions are of significant complexity, they may likewise be decomposed to provide more detail.

As shown in Figure 2.21, additional decisions must be made in order to select a mode of transportation. These include:

- Determining the available modes of shipment. For example, at higher weights and volumes, rail and barge intermodal shipments become feasible options.

- Selecting insurance coverage for the shipment. Internal governance might require that the transportation of higher risk materials requires additional liability insurance above the coverage offered by the carrier.

- Determining transportation cost. When several modes of transportation are an option, all costs are computed so that the lowest cost option can be selected.

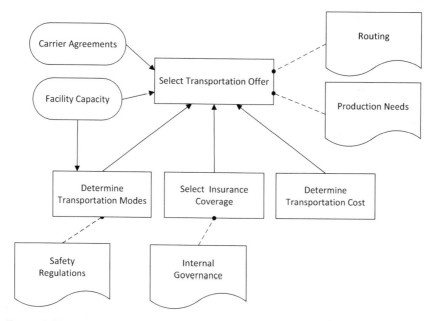

Figure 2.21　*A decision requirements diagram showing an initial decomposition.*

As this additional detail is added, it may also be useful to add additional input data or knowledge source elements that are required by these decisions. The information requirements to input data and the authority requirements to knowledge sources already identified may also need to change. Frequently, authority requirements are moved from the initial decision participating in the association to a sub-decision as it becomes clearer what the authority requirements affect.

These diagrams can be an interim step toward a more complete set of decision requirements, or they can be a destination in their own right, especially for a manual decision where this level of description is often enough.

Complete Requirements

When complete requirements are required for a decision, such as when the whole decision is going to be automated, a decision requirements diagram can be used to show the complete requirements. Additional decision, input data, and knowledge sources can be added and linked using information and authority requirements.

In such a diagram, it is important that the information represented by each input data and produced by each decision is correctly described in terms of a hierarchical information model. This represents the information that flows through the decision network.

Although decision logic is not necessarily specified for the whole diagram (see later chapters for more on how to define decision logic), it may be apparent that there will be some reusable blocks of decision logic. These can be represented using business knowledge models that are linked to the decision or decisions that use the logic using knowledge requirement links. The most common use case will be where two or more decisions, with different (but compatible) Information Requirements, share the same decision logic and are therefore linked to a common business knowledge model. For example, two decisions might validate the address on an invoice and the address on a purchase order, respectively. These are different input data, which means these decisions are different. However, they will likely share a common set of address validation logic represented as a business knowledge model. Business knowledge models might also be added to clarify knowledge management issues or be used as placeholders for analytic models or other algorithms.

Subset Requirements

Because DMN allows many diagrams to be defined for a single Decision Requirements Model it is entirely appropriate to use diagrams to represent subsets of the overall requirements. As many or as few such diagrams can be developed, allowing, for instance, a diagram that shows only the elements of a diagram of interest to a particular business unit or only the decision network without input data or knowledge sources. The standard does not define a notation to show that there is missing data or requirements, which could be shown on the diagram because one or both ends of the requirement are present. Nevertheless, it is generally good practice to clearly identify those diagrams that are not meant to show the current complete understanding of the problem.

Other Diagrams

In principle, all sorts of possible diagrams can be defined: – those that only show input data, diagrams focused only on business knowledge models and their interactions, or every element owned by a particular business unit. As long as the purpose and intended completeness of each such diagram is clear, these can be extremely useful.

USING THE BASIC SHAPES

With this understanding of the basic shapes, modelers can start building a diagram for a process model, including one that uses a decision model. Typical processes, such as supply chain management and contract management, will serve as business examples for the rest of this chapter. For example, in detailing a portion of the process where the contracting office awards a bid to a contractor, the steps include advertising, bid evaluation, and bid award. Intuitively, these are the activities in the process. Figure 2.22 shows BPMN for this portion of a process's flow of activities, including the start and top events.

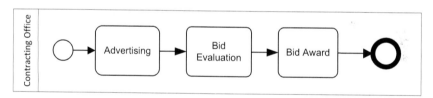

Figure 2.22 *Sequence flow within the contracting office.*

In the first scenario, a decision Bid Evaluation that would be useful to model in DMN has already been identified. As the process is modeled, the user can look for decisions in the descriptive elements.

Advertising and bids suggest there is communication ongoing, so the modeler might add messages to the contractor and to the model, as shown in Figure 2.23.

In the next related scenario, a requisition for material is being sourced. Through modeling, analysts record the group's understanding of activities and their relationships in the process. For example, they might observe organizational activities and dependencies. In the requisition example in Figure 2.24, the ana-

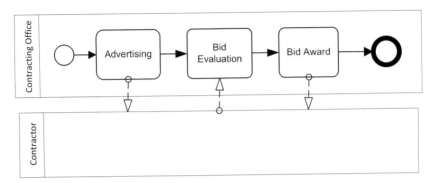

Figure 2.23 *Message flow between the contractor and the contracting office.*

lysts observe that sourcing transportation and submitting the order can be parallel tasks, and therefore the parallel gateway should be used.

Figure 2.24 shows a parallel split flow arising in a sequence flow. In parallel branches, process flow might move through any number of activities, and the activities can be in any of the states that were described above. Branches might merge, or other branches might finish while other activities might continue to advance through the process.

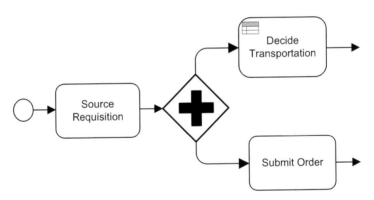

Figure 2.24 *Simple parallel split with parallel gateway and a DMN decision.*

As shown in figure 2.25, the parallel split also shows the first place where several tokens might be considered. A sequence was defined as the passing of a single token. When two sequences left the gateway after the Source Requisition activity, two tokens were generated. These tokens need to be consumed when the process is completed.

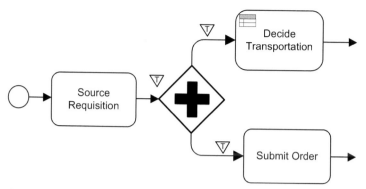

Figure 2.25 *Parallel gateway split with tokens.*

The decision model for transportation should be completed and included in the model. Figure 2.26 shows a more complete model of the transportation decision.

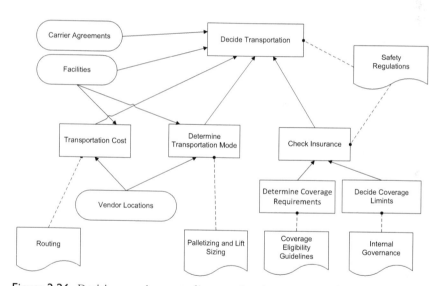

Figure 2.26 *Decision requirements diagram showing more complete requirements.*

- To determine the available modes of shipment, a facilities capability feeds into the ability to receive a mode of shipment, such as rail.
- To select insurance coverage for the shipment, additional decisions are needed for coverage requirements and the limits on liability amounts.
- To determine transportation cost agreements with the carriers, routes and locations are all considered.

The overall transportation decision then feeds into the process through the business rules task.

To complete the scenario, we receive and inspect the items and determine if the items can be placed into inventory or returned. This process fragment was already covered so it can be appended to the diagram. However, the parallel gateway must first be merged. The either/or nature of the defect implies an exclusive gateway and a return. Figure 2.27 shows the entire scenario.

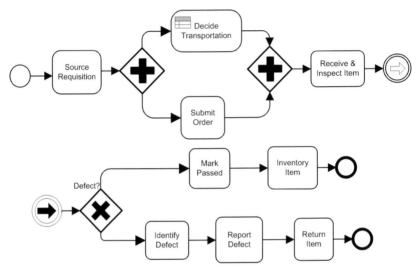

Figure 2.27 *Complete scenario, including the inspection. The white arrow and black arrow are connecting events and represent a continuation of the process.*

SUMMARY

The first part of the chapter presented a basic pallet of shapes that every BPMN and DMN designer should know by heart. All but the most complex process and design scenarios can be modeled with these shapes for the happy path route.

Next, the basics of activities, gateways, and events in BPMN were reviewed. A BPMN process is a flow of data and tokens through elements and across time that follow a data-dependent course according to the values of the data. The motion of data takes place in messages, sequences, and activities. Understanding how the elements affect the flow of the tokens is critical for deciding how to model a scenario. It was established that the activity moves through three states: ready, active, and completed.

In BPMN, a gateway directs the flow of a process. There are three basic gateways: the data-based exclusive gateway, the parallel gateway, and the data-based inclusive gateway. At the merge, all gateways wait for the proper quantity of tokens to arrive.

The data-based exclusive (remember *x-clusive* for the *x* in the diamond) gateway is activated by a single token, even if multiple sequences point toward the shape. A data condition passes the single token.

The parallel gateway waits for all active sequences to finish their work and pass their tokens. At the split, tokens are generated unconditionally for every exiting sequence.

Like the parallel gateway, the inclusive gateway (remember *or* for the o shown in the diamond) waits for all active sequences to finish their work and pass their tokens. At the split, tokens are generated conditionally for every leaving sequence.

Events are denoted by circles. Starting events are denoted by thin lines; intermediate events, by double lines; and end events, by thick lines. These notations hold true for all events in BPMN.

Figure 2.28 summarizes this chapter's BPMN-related topics.

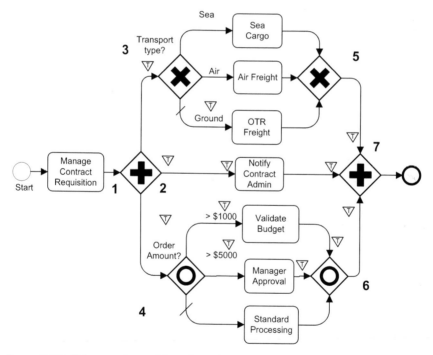

Figure 2.28 *Tokens and transitions from the basic palette.*

Here is the timeline of the process in Figure 2.28:

1. A single token leaves Manage Contract Requisition; the output data will be used in the gateways. The single token enters the parallel gateway.
2. Three paths and token emerge from the parallel gateway.
3. A single token activates the data-based exclusive gateway. The default transport type is chosen, and the token is passed along that path.
4. The inclusive gateway is activated (in parallel with Path 3), and because the amount is greater than $5,000, the two top sequences are chosen.
5. When the OTR Freight activity is completed, the token is passed to the exclusive merge and is immediately passed to the parallel merge gateway. The parallel gateway will wait for all the tokens to arrive before activating.
6. The inclusive gateway will wait for the Validate Budget and Manager Approval activities to complete and pass a single token to the downstream gateway.
7. Once the parallel gateway receives the three tokens, it will consume them and send a single token to the end event.

A process model in BPMN is more than paths on a workflow diagram; it is a depiction of what happens on an element-by-element basis. Various elements have requirements for activation, and most of them require at least one token, as well as input data. Activities, subprocesses and gateways go through specific states, and the BPMN specification describes how these affect execution.

The elements of BPMN follow a repeating pattern: they transition through states, and they raise exceptions and conditions. For process modelers, it is important to know the combinations of tokens, which are the conditions that activate the elements, when learning the elements of BPMN. This will simplify understanding what the more complex shapes do.

This chapter also set out the core elements of the Decision Model and Notation standard—decisions, input data, knowledge sources, and business knowledge models—and described the three kinds of requirement dependencies that can be drawn between them, which are information requirements, authority requirements, and knowledge requirements. These elements can be combined into decision requirements diagrams to describe the decision making at various levels of detail.

Decision requirements diagrams are used to accurately specify how manual decisions in a process should be made and to specify requirements for decision automation using a business rules management system or similar tool. They break down decision making into its component pieces for clarity and to allow automation boundaries to be specified. They show what information is required to make each part of the decision, as well as where the rules, guidelines, policies, and know-how to make the decision correctly can be found.

Decision modeling is a relatively new approach for most organizations. This chapter provides the tools for users to read decision models and represent decision models in a standard way as decision modeling is developed as a discipline alongside process modeling. Knowing the notation for decision models is necessary for decision modeling, but just as with process modeling, the notation is not a methodology, and developing effective models will likely take practice and training.

CHAPTER 3

BUILDING ON THE BASICS

In Chapter 2, the basics of BPMN/DMN were discussed. In addition to modeling decisions and the paths a process travels, the chapter also detailed that process modeling in BPMN has a dynamic side that describes a time-dependent passing of data along sequences represented by tokens. A particular set of tokens must arrive in order for gateway and activity shapes to be activated. Once activated, a gateway or activity follows a predictable pattern that is denoted by the shape's decoration. In this chapter we will build on this with more BPMN elements.

Chapter 2 also discussed DMN and how to model decisions. This chapter introduces the addition of business logic to decision models, as well as defining some additional properties that are worth capturing to document decisions and decision models.

This chapter also covers the event-oriented features of BPMN, especially message events. Messaging is a prominent feature of BPMN models, and messaging is implemented as events and tasks. Messages are the mechanism for pools and processes to communicate. The adoption of Event-Driven Architecture (EDA) has evolved the practice of process modeling (see Chapter 5), and BPMN is especially designed to be event-driven and therefore respond to EDA.

A business process is dynamic and must allow for and perhaps recover from unpredictable circumstances. As such, BPMN allows the process flow to be triggered or altered by events both inside and outside the organization. Internally, events might be the reassignment of an employee, the change of budget items, or the issue of new guidelines and directives. Externally, these events can be transactions, such as notices and communications with customers, partners, and government entities. They can also include environmental, political, or economic data such as news, weather, water quality, or commodity prices.

As the focus of process modeling dives into the details of a process, models will need the ability to loop through records, time, and conditions.

BPMN elements build complexity by adding capabilities to base elements. That turns the simple event into a timer event by virtue of the addition of an interior clock. For most elements, events, gateways, and activities, the attributes of the inner element inherit the attributes of the outer elements, becoming a composite of all the attributes. Figure 3.1 reflects this idea in a timer event.

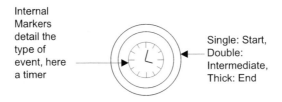

Figure 3.1 *BPMN event syntax.*

The graphical elements suggest functionality, and data attributes control the behavior of the elements. This chapter will review a number of these composites, including composites of activity types and gateways.

An effective model is both descriptive and concise, using detailed words and clear elements. Yet drawing out every detail in perfect BPMN syntax might not always be sufficient. BPMN includes features that are useful for documentation. This chapter will also introduce other shapes and modeling styles that might be helpful to model more details about processes and decisions.

MORE ACTIVITIES AND TASKS

As process modeling delves into deeper details, business and operational particulars will become clearer. The following activities and tasks model these deeper requirements.

Specific Task Types

The BPMN 2.0 specification adds six subtypes to tasks. The composite variations generally add metadata that relate to the nominal characteristics of the task. They also provide more detail on the execution characteristics of the process.

Often, in the early phases of modeling a process, many details are unknown, including participants and the characteristics of the system architecture that will execute the task. A good practice is to describe the happy path activity flow for the entire process first before attempting to identify who or what performs the tasks. Any involved activities should be defined before identifying who or what completes the activity. Subsequently, these specific activity types are useful for refining process discovery and documentation.

Table 3.1 Task Shapes Designated for a Specific Purpose

Receive Message Task Task involves asynchronous interaction with another participant.	The white envelope denotes that the task will not be complete until a message is received. A received message should be attached.	Message Task
Send Message Task Task involves interaction with another participant.	The dark envelope denotes that the task immediately sends a message. A sent message should be attached.	Message Task
Manual Task Task is performed manually outside the scope of a BPM System (BPMS) or software application such as a Customer Relationship Management (CRM) or Enterprise Resource Planning (ERP) system.	Manual tasks are not managed by the engine and have no effect on execution. They immediately transition to completion and have no sent or received messages.	Manual Task
Human Task Task is performed by a person. This is typically used in a BPMS to differentiate form-based and system tasks.	The human task generally works with a task list that manages the visibility of the task according to the role of the user.	Human Task
Service Task Task is synchronously performed by a system service.	For legacy reasons, these can be visualized as an interaction with a web service. Sent and received messages can be attached to the service task.	Service Task
Script Task Represents a software script that runs automatically when the task is activated.	This changes the values of input data objects in a programming language such as Xpath, Jscript, or Visual Basic(.net) that the engine understands.	Script Task
Rule Task Represents an activity where business rules will determine the activity outcome.	This is a placeholder for (business rule-driven) decisions and is the natural placeholder for a DMN decision task.	Rule Task

To expand on a DMN integration example, Figure 3.2 shows an example with the message, rule, and script shapes and gateways. Subsequent chapters will delve deeply into this.

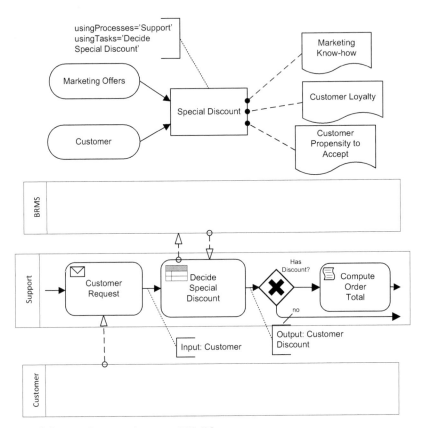

Figure 3.2 *DMN connections to a BPMN process.*

The customer request message moves customer data as input to Decide Special Discount. This rule task executes logic associated with the business knowledge pertaining to the special discount decision modeling in DMN. The business logic is implemented in a BRMS. The logic in the BRMS returns the discount, and a script applies the discount.

In DMN 1.0, a process is connected to a decision by metadata. Decisions can be associated with one or more business processes to indicate that the decision is made during those processes. Decisions can also be associated with one or more specific tasks, usually business rules tasks, within those processes to indicate that the tasks involve making the decision at that specific point in the process.

Figure 3.2 shows a public process with a customer participant. Either message is attached to the boundary, or only those activities that are used to communicate to the other participant are included in the public process. Process models do not always need to show the interaction details of participants. The focus of the diagram might be a single participant; however, the model might detail the points of interaction. The pool can define the other participant involvement without details of the activities. This is commonly used for an external participant, such as a vendor, supplier, or other third-party organization.

Note that there is no notation to show how a DMN decision requirements diagram is linked to a BPMN process diagram. Text annotations are typically used for this purpose, as shown.

Figure 3.3 illustrates a sample process that shows the proper usage of the send, receive, script, and human tasks.

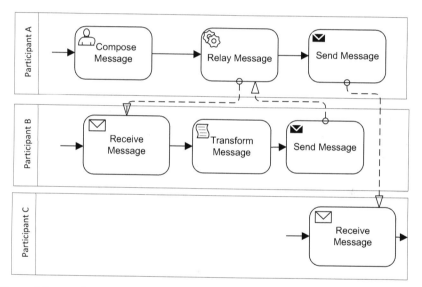

Figure 3.3 *An abstract use case to remember the role of activity types.*

Participant A uses a form in Compose a Message and forwards this to the Relay Message service task, which in turn sends a message to participant B. The Transform Message script task uses code, such as XPath, to change the message. The message is returned to participant A. Subsequently, the send message task forwards the transformed message to participant C.

As the notation implies, a message task cannot simultaneously send and receive a message. Sending and receiving a message can be done with a single service, two message tasks, or two intermediate message events. The event section of this chapter discusses the message event further.

Iterations and Multiplicity

As modeling focuses on the details of a process, models will need the ability to loop through records, time, and conditions.

An activity that repeats for multiple iterations is called a *looping activity.* Looping activities can be either a task or a subprocess. The marker for the looping task or subprocess is a pointed arc. This means that the activity has the looping characteristic.

Looping Task

Looping Subprocess

The looping task is a basic activity performed repeatedly. For example, a procedure repeats until a condition is met. More often, looping activities are subprocesses. Because it is a compound, multi-step activity, a looping subprocess can apply a subprocess to a set of records. A purchase order might have multiple products to be sourced and delivered. When the loop ends, the activity is completed, and the process continues to the next activity.

The loop is dependent on a condition. For example, the condition could be, "Continue looping until the document is approved or rejected," as in Figure 3.4. The three conditions or characteristics of the loop are:

1.   Loop for a number of times, called the loop counter.
2.   Loop while a condition exists.
3.   Loop until the condition exits.

There is nothing that explicitly shows the loop characteristic; however, it is part of the BPMN data model. A text annotation might be used to describe the loop stopping condition. Annotations will be covered in a later chapter.

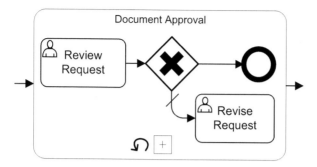

Figure 3.4 *Looping subprocess (expanded).*

In Figure 3.4, a manager has a set of documents to review. The loop will iterate until the list of documents is completed.

Multiple-Instance Subprocess

Another looping activity type is the *multiple-instance subprocess*. The purpose of this is to create a number of instances to process an input data source with the process flow located within the subprocess. The instances may execute in parallel or may be sequential. The multi-instance subprocess can manage four scenarios:

1. The activities in the subprocess should execute in a fixed number of parallel instances. The number can always be set programmatically.
2. The activities in the subprocess should execute in a fixed number of sequential instances.
3. The activities in the subprocess should execute across a collection in parallel. The number of parallel instances is determined by the collection count.
4. The activities in the subprocess should execute across a collection in sequence. The number of sequential instances is determined by the collection count.

The number of instances in the first two cases can be calculated by an expression assigned to the count by the process. This type of loop can be configured to control the tokens produced..

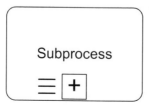

Multiple-instance subprocess: Serial execution

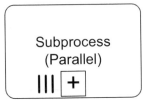

Multiple-instance subprocess: Parallel execution

In the first two scenarios above, the subprocess would take advantage of a multi-processor environment to apply computing resources to the procedure. When concurrent execution is faster or more efficient among multiple participants, parallelism can optimize a process. A listener that is handling queues of requests can start multiple instances.

In the second case, the subprocess can manage a collection or list of business objects including shipments, receipts, change requests, and chain of custody reports. Here, the count of the collection would drive the instance count. For example, a multiple-instance activity could be used for an order sourcing process with a collection of 10 order items that must be filled.

In contrast to these four scenarios, the looping subprocess might denote an indeterminate continuation. If the condition never arrives, the cycles would execute indefinitely.

The parallel version of the multiple-instance subprocess is used when all activities should be completed in parallel. Figure 3.5 shows a process with a parallel multiple-instance simultaneously sending and processing a commercial offering from each person out of a group of people.

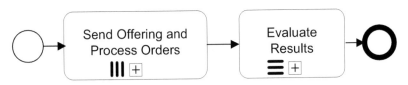

Figure 3.5 *A contrast of serial and parallel multiple-instance.*

Requirements such as iterating through a stack of documents might call for a serial, multiple-instance subprocess. For example, a participant receives five documents that must be signed. The documents can only be signed one at a time (sequentially) and must be kept in order. Therefore, this would impose serial execution. The discerning factor is whether or not a sequence is needed for iterations. Figure 3.5 shows the offer being evaluated with a serial multiple-instance. After all orders have been processed, a single participant will evaluate the order, once for each order received.

Consider the requirement, "For each customer in the Southeast, send a promotional email." When the number of customers in the criteria is fixed, use the serial multiple-instances, instead of the looping subprocess. In contrast, the looping subprocess is more likely a do-while or do-until loop type. Do-while and do-until loop types typically lack a predetermined iteration count. An approval process continues to ask for revisions until the item is either approved or rejected (do-until).

Looping without the Looping Subprocess

There are ways to illustrate looping processes in BPMN without one of the looping subprocesses. The most common is called *upstream flow*. Here the flow routes back (upstream) or to a previously executed activity. Figure 3.6 shows an example of upstream flow. This style of modeling can be used with multiple lanes inside a single pool.

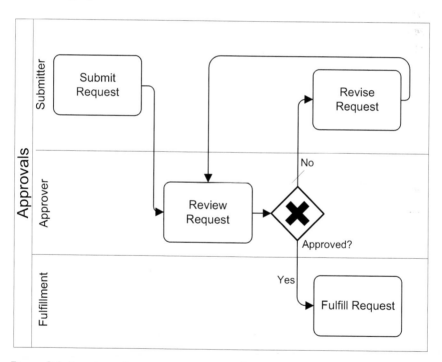

Figure 3.6 *Looping using upstream sequence flow.*

Often, a looping subprocess is a better choice because it shows a repeating behavior. There are advantages and disadvantages to using the upstream flow method of looping (Figure 3.19). While drawing lines in various directions can be difficult to follow, this simplified notation can be more understandable. Often, a looping subprocess is a better choice because it shows a repeating behavior instead of a repetitive redoing of the results.

ADVANCED EVENTS

Message Event

There are five basic types of message events: start, non-interrupting start, intermediate, non-interrupting intermediate, and end. Boundary events can act on the border of a subprocess. Like the empty start, intermediate, and end shapes, the thin line, double line, and thick line mark where different message events can be used within a process flow. Dashed lines for the non-interrupting process are used on a subprocess boundary. .

Table 3.2 The six basic BPMN message events

Event Type	BPMN
Start	
Non-Interrupting Start	
Intermediate Receiving	
Non-Interrupting Intermediate	
Intermediate Sending	
Ending Sending	

The message shapes display an envelope icon or marker in the center. Each inherits the rules of the corresponding empty start, intermediate, and end event shapes. The start shape event is used at the beginning of a process diagram and has no sequence flow lines entering it. The end event shape, by definition, cannot have any sequence flow leaving.

Message start events (white envelope) receive messages, denoted by the sharp arrowhead pointing at the shape. Message end events (dark envelope) send messages, with the blunt end of the message line attached to the shape. In BPMN, white shapes are catching events, and dark shapes are throwing events.

Throwing and Catching Events

The term *throwing* means *sending*, and *catching* means *receiving*. There are a number of event shapes that throw and catch an event. An event is thrown when the event condition is triggered. An event is caught by the shape designated to handle the thrown condition. Message events are displayed with a filled icon sending, and the message (and the unfilled icon) receiving.

The throwing and catching pattern of filled and empty exists with the other event shapes. Filled icons specify an event thrower (sends), and unfilled icons specify an event catcher (receives).

Intermediate events can be attached to the boundary of a subprocess. These are known intermediate boundary events. In the case of messages, something inside the subprocess throws a message, and it is caught on the boundary of the process. Using an end message prevents any tokens from remaining behind.

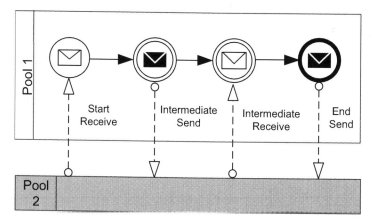

Figure 3.7 *Examples of the four types of messages interacting with a public pool.*

Figure 3.8 shows two pools representing two participants. First, the empty start event shape in the pool labeled Contract Officer shows the start of the process. A subprocess containing a human task prepares a message and throws the

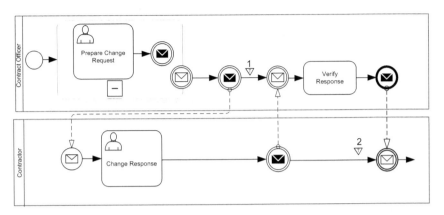

Figure 3.8 *Use of message events between participants. The process is complete when the message in the top pool is sent.*

message to a catching, intermediate subprocess event. From the Contractor perspective, a process instance starts when a message is received from the Contract Officer. Before this event, the Contractor is not involved in this process.

At Points 1 and 2 on the diagram, the token will advance to the intermediate receiving task and await the arrival of the message before activating the next sequence.

In general, a message start event starts when a message triggers the event. A token is generated and transitions to the next step (Change Response) in the example process. The message might be an unqualified trigger signal that starts the process, or it may include process data. In the context of this process, the message contains a requested contract change that the contractor reviews in a human task.

From the perspective of the participant represented by each pool, the intermediate message events indicate the wait state of an event on a sequence until receipt of messages from the other participant. A token would arrive at the intermediate event and await the arrival of the message. The ending for the Contract Officer participant in Figure 3.8 is a message end event.

There are important rules for modeling with message events:

- A start message event exclusively receives messages.
- An end message event exclusively sends a message.
- An intermediate message event can either send or receive a message.
- When a message is being received in an intermediate event, use the empty envelope (white). When a message is being sent, use the filled envelope (black).

Additionally, a process instance might wait for information from other participants to continue at multiple intermediate message events. Depending on the data received, there might be multiple outcomes or multiple end events.

Earlier, we discussed the use of the message events or an activity that sends a message. It can be difficult to determine if a task or an event should be used. To make the proper choice, the message interaction must be classified as synchronous or asynchronous.

> *Synchronous Messaging:* Here the activity requests information from another participant and the message sender must wait for a response before continuing. This is also known as message blocking. Synchronous messaging is typically depicted in BPMN as a service task.
>
> An example of this is when a courier delivers a package and requires a signature. The package will not be delivered unless there is an acknowledgement that the package was received. Another example is in system-to-system communication: as part of a transaction, the remote system sends an acknowledgement.
>
> *Asynchronous Messaging:* The activity requests information from another participant. However, the message sender is not required to wait for an immediate response. Instead, the sender can do something else, and the recipient will eventually return a response. Asynchronous messaging is typically depicted in BPMN with two message events: one for sending and the other for receiving.

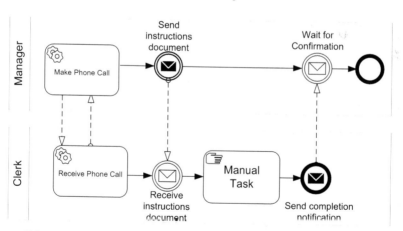

Figure 3.9 *Usage of tasks and events for messaging. The Make Phone Call is a synchronous activity, and the service is used, while the events are not.*

In Figure 3.9, the Manager first makes a phone call. This is actually a manual event; however, it is used as an analogy for synchronous messaging because it involves an interactive conversation. During the conversation, the manager cannot do anything else. Because the process is blocked from continuing until the task is complete, synchronous messaging is also referred to as blocking.

In the conversation, the manager informs the clerk of the task at hand and to expect a document and instructions. The conversation is complete, so the tasks for both participants are complete. Next, the manager sends the document. Between the phone conversation and the receipt of the document, the clerk might be doing something else. It is likely the clerk will react to the receipt of the document according to the priority set by the manager. Similarly, when the document is sent, the manager could be doing something else. But when the manager receives confirmation, his process is now active again.

The manual task is a placeholder for documenting an expected activity. However, it has no effect on the execution of the process. The token will pass through the manual event unimpeded.

Timer Events

The *timer* event is one of the versatile shapes in BPMN. It expresses a time interval in processing or a wait for a time, or it triggers actions on overdue events, activities, or other processes. The timer events include the start and intermediate events, but there is no timer end event. The start and intermediate events appear as shown.

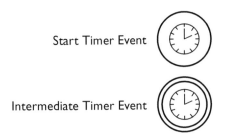

In Figure 3.10, the Start Timer Event shows that a process starts in a given time period. For example, the system runs a report on the last day of each month.

Figure 3.10 *A time-driven report.*

A specified time could be a given day such as every Friday, the last day of the month, or the first day of each quarter. A time such as two hours or three days could also be specified. The time event has settable input attributes, which can be developed by upstream decisions. The decision would use multiple logic steps and data to decide optimal frequencies for processes activities or exceptions.

The intermediate timer event in Figure 3.11 expresses a process wait for a period before continuing. Like the timer start shape, the period may be expressed in an interval's duration, or it may be a calendar date.

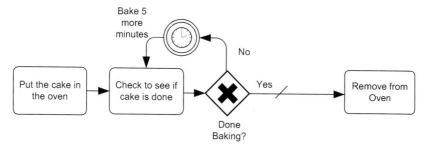

Figure 3.11 *A timer event used as an intermediate event.*

The intermediate timer event expresses actions taken when something is not done within a certain period, which means an alternate action such as an escalation path is desired.

Figure 3.12 shows an intermediate boundary timing event. In subprocesses, the intermediate event catches a timeout condition. This is another example of a subprocess shape with an intermediate event attached to the border of the subprocess. The alternate path starts in Figure 3.12 when the employee does not complete the work within the allotted duration

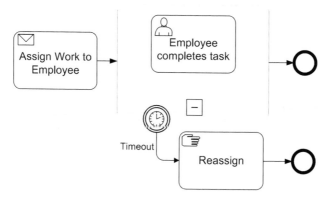

Figure 3.12 *Timer event used as an intermediate event.*

Scope Cancellation and Non-Interrupting Events

Some modeling scenarios might call for a flow of activities that do not interrupt the sequence flow within the parent subprocess. For example, after a period of inactivity, the process requests a status check without cancelling the current activity. Figure 3.13 introduces a timer event that does not interrupt the subprocess flow.

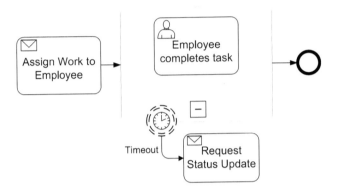

Figure 3.13 *Non-interrupting timer event.*

The timer event in Figure 3.13 is intermediate, but with one variation. The dashed lines on the intermediate event indicate events that do not interrupt the parent subprocess. Non-interrupting events can only be used on a subprocess border.

Multiple events can be attached to the border of a subprocess. As the diagram for the previous example develops, it might be determined that a timer is inadequate. For instance, when a message is received from an external source, the subprocess might need to be explicitly cancelled.

In Figure 3.14, the other intermediate message event cancels the parent subprocess. The timer does not. The timer is triggered after a period and prompts the manager to check the status of the employee activity. If the cancellation message is received, the employee's activity is discontinued. Because the employee task was delegated, a notification is sent, informing the employee to stop working on this process instance.

Conditional Events

The *conditional event* is a bit more sophisticated than the timer and message events. Timers are triggered by time, and messages are triggered once a participant sends a message. A conditional event is somewhat more automated and

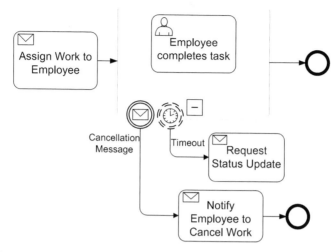

Figure 3.14 *Multiple events on the subprocess border.*

assumes an active system mechanism, such as an event processing platform, to trigger the condition.

Here, three of the conditional event varieties will be described: start, intermediate, and intermediate non-interrupting. The non-interrupting start will be covered in the next chapter. Figure 3.15 shows an example of the condition start event in use.

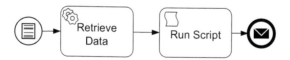

Figure 3.15 *Condition start event triggers an automated process.*

Scenarios employing the conditional event often employ decisions or can be replaced with an event timer and a rule/BRMS-based decision. When the condition for a conditional event gets very complex, it might be better to trigger a decision with a timer, decide if the condition has occurred (using a true/false decision model), and then conditionally generate a message.

It is possible to use the conditional event in human-centric processes. A condition event can be placed on the activity border when the activity has not completed and an interrupting condition arises or is discovered (Figure 3.16).

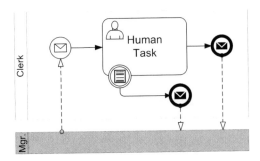

Figure 3.16 *Condition event interrupting a human task.*

Without driving data or triggering events, condition events do not arise. Also, a participant must subsequently evaluate the condition. In Figure 3.16, a system facility likely monitors activity and triggers the start.

Alternately, the condition event can suggest a hidden or off-diagram participant. In Figure 3.16, if the participant were a person, how does the participant receive the data and events to evaluate the condition? This point is not evident by assessing the diagram. Therefore, in some cases, another event shape, such as the signal event, should be used instead.

Signal Event

Signal events are depicted by triangles inside circles. There are six types of signal events and corresponding symbols. Five are shown in Table 3.3.

The sixth signal, the non-interrupting start signal, will be covered in the next chapter.

The signal pattern is like a radio broadcast. Ordinary message shapes send a message from one participant to another. Yet the process might need to send messages to a group of listening participants. The receiving group might even be uncertain. The signal message continuously broadcasts, and those who want to listen to the broadcast tune in or subscribe.

The signal event can broadcast to all processes simultaneously. The signal intermediate (throwing) and signal end shapes denote this broadcast. The signal start and signal intermediate (catching) events allow an activity to receive a broadcast.

Signal events can also be used for synchronization between parallel branches. In Figure 3.17, activities A1 and B1 begin at the same time. However, B2 cannot begin before A1 is complete. Messages cannot be sent to the same participant in the same pool. Because all participants can potentially receive signals, they can be used in the same pool.

A process might make another broadcast after A2 in Figure 3.17. The signal after B1 could receive either signal from the A branch. Again, the process could be stopped because B1 might take longer to complete than A1 and A2 combined.

Table 3.3 Five types of signal events

Event Type	BPMN
Start Signal Event	
Intermediate Signal Event	
Intermediate Signal Event (catching, non-interrupting)	
Intermediate Signal Event (throwing)	
End Signal Event	

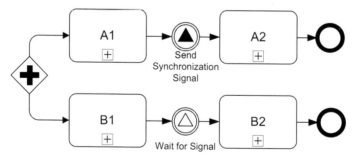

Figure 3.17 *Use of signals for synchronization.*

The addition of the parallel split and merge in Figure 3.18 ensures that A1, B1, and A2, B2 are kept in synch.

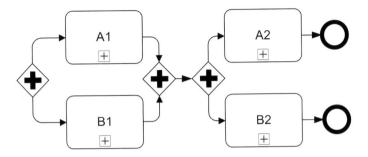

Figure 3.18 *Using parallel merge instead of signals.*

Here is a comparison of the different types of events:

- Messages are used for point-to-point communication between participants when it is desired to show where interactions exist. Guaranteed message receipt is desired.

- Signals are used for communications where a relevant participant might or might not exist. The signal sender is not necessarily aware of any specific recipients. Signals are typically used to notify interested participants of changing data or processing states. Message receipt confirmation is not desired because it would generate too much overhead.

- Conditions are used to detect a possible combination of criteria from multiple sources. A participant is responsible for detecting its own condition criteria because no notification of changing criteria exists.

Link Event

The link event is a bit of a misnomer. The *link event* is a diagramming mechanism for breaking and continuing sequence flows. This might also be thought of as a go-to for a process model. There are two types of link events, intermediate catching and intermediate throwing, as shown here.

The link denotes a break in a sequence flow. Therefore, there is no start or end event. If a diagram page is to start with a link event, then the catching (unfilled) intermediate link event should be used.

Because it is a break in a sequence, the link shape marks a continuation point of a process. Therefore, only the intermediate link shapes make sense.

Figure 3.19 shows the proper usage of the link events. The process can be started by any start event. Alternately, the process can continue from this point with the intermediate link event (catching). The gateway makes a decision to either continue in this diagram or continue on another diagram with the intermediate link event (throwing).

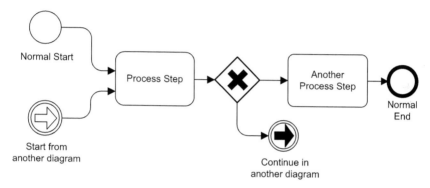

Figure 3.19 *Link event usage.*

The link event can be used to jump to another point in a diagram where it might be difficult to follow the thin line of an interaction. Therefore, links are often used instead of drawing lines because it creates a much cleaner diagram.

Figure 3.20 illustrates a hiring process which finds 10 candidates and does initial telephone screenings. If the candidates have the necessary skills, they move to the interview subprocess. Sometimes, after speaking with the first 10 candidates, not enough are found to start interviewing. If this is the case, the gateway "Enough to interview?" routes to "No," leading to the link event. The link points back to point A.

The candidate search is conducted in parallel with multiple recruiters (note the parallel marker on the multi-instance subprocess). However, the actual interview process occurs in a series, one after the other. The number of candidates is predetermined before the subprocess starts, so the multiple-instance serial sub-

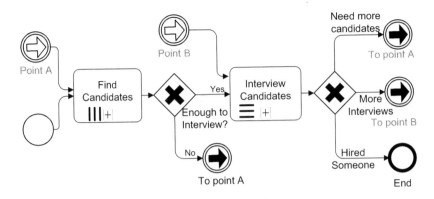

Figure 3.20 *Using link events instead of lines.*

process is used. After the first round of interviews, there could be one of three different outcomes:

1. All candidates might have been eliminated. In Figure 3.20, this would cause the second gateway to route to the link event, directing back to point A.

2. There might be a protocol to interview candidates more than once to help with the decision process. The second gateway in Figure 3.20 would route to the link event that routes to point B.

3. In the default outcome, someone was hired, and the process is complete.

Multiple Events and Multiple Parallel Events

There are a number of scenarios where one of a number or a combination of events will start or complete an intermediate point in a process. For example, a process might start with a phone call or an online application. More typically, different channels or services, having different forms, will trigger a single event. For this scenario, BPMN has included the multiple and parallel events.

A multiple event is started or activated when one of the triggering events occurs, in the case of starting or intermediate, or when there are multiple outcomes for the end of a process. Because a single event triggers the event, these are exclusive forms. Parallel events are similar; however, all the events in the sequence must occur for the event to activate.

Intermediate tasks can be added to the boundary of subprocesses. There are non-interrupting starting forms of these that will be covered in the next chapter.

A multiple event is a mechanism for controlling a process with multiple triggering events. Triggers could include messages, timers, conditions, signals, escalations, and other event types. Escalations and signals are covered later in this book. First, the general purpose of the multiple event is introduced, and then some of

Table 3.4 Multiple Event and Multiple Parallel Event Types

Event Type	Activation Requirements	Multiple Event	Multiple Parallel Event
Start	For multiple, one event activates; for parallel, all must occur to start.		
Intermediate	For multiple, one event activates or catches the trigger; for parallel, all start.		
Intermediate	Throwing, all events are thrown, no parallel equivalent.		N/A
Non-Interrupting	One event activates or catches the trigger; for parallel, all events must catch the trigger.		
End Event	All events are thrown, no parallel equivalent		N/A

the complex use cases are examined. Figure 3.25 illustrates an example of using multiple events.

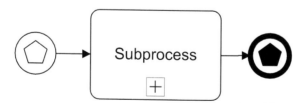

Figure 3.21 *Drawing generic events with multiple shapes.*

Importantly, any of the possible events could trigger the start event. Since one event triggers the transition, this is "exclusive" behavior.

The end event in Figure 3.25 could throw multiple events, and it throws all events that apply.

Event-Based Exclusive Gateway

In Chapter 2, data-based gateways were introduced. Data-based gateways evaluate a data condition to select a sequence flow path. For example, "Hire the candidate?" could have answers such as "yes," "no," and "maybe." With event-based gateways, the selection is based on an event, often arriving in a message. Figure 3.22 provides an example of handling multiple events from one gateway.

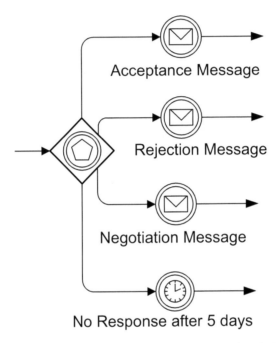

Acceptance Message

Rejection Message

Negotiation Message

No Response after 5 days

Figure 3.22 *Multiple events on an intermediate, event-based exclusive gateway.*

If a process is to start upon receiving one of multiple starting messages, perhaps with different data types, then the event-driven exclusive gateway with intermediate message events should be used.

As shown in Figures 3.23 and 3.24, the event-driven exclusive gateway is a diamond shape with either an inner start (single line) or an inner intermediate event shape (double thin line). As the shape implies, the event-driven gateway shape is a composite of both the data-based exclusive gateway and the multiple event start.

The event-driven exclusive gateway awaits a single message or event. Events include regular messages, signals, and timers. Usually, messages and events occur before process gateways, so the notation may seem backwards. However, event shapes are drawn on the right side of the event-driven gateway or downstream.

Figure 3.23 *Event-driven gateway symbol (start).*

Figure 3.24 *Event-driven gateway symbol (intermediate).*

Placing the events on the left (upstream) side would be a series of events converging at the gateway.

The event-driven exclusive gateway can come in the start of a process or in a sequence as an intermediate shape. When the gateway is at the start of the process, the event shape inside the diamond is the multiple start event, a single thin line. Figure 3.25 shows the use of the event-driven gateway at the start of a process.

The gateway shape is a substitute for a start event. It awaits the activation of the downstream event shapes. In most process scenarios, one defined starting point exists, but with this gateway, a process can start in multiple ways.

When used as the start event, the event-based exclusive gateway indicates a new process instance for each event. In Figure 3.25, the receipt of a fax will create one process instance. A subsequent receipt of an email on the gateway would start a different process instance, separate from the instance started by the fax message.

In Figure 3.25, three different event shapes can activate the merging gateway. One option is for an email message event to start a process. There is a corresponding activity, Transfer Data. Once an intermediate message is received and the process instance starts, it merges back into a people or systems process. Through one of three possible message types, the process initializes. Each message type requires different processing activities.

Another use case can also demonstrate the power of the event driven gateway. The first activity in Figure 3.26, Call External System, awaits an answer from an external system. A message gateway awaits the system's response. The external system may be owned by another organization and controlled by its resources. There is rationale for separating system responses. A delay period occurs between sending and receiving the request. This is also an asynchronous interaction.

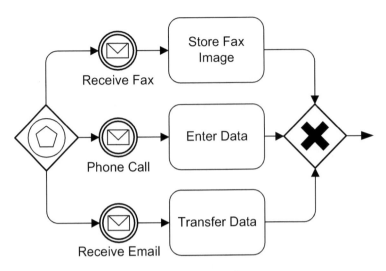

Figure 3.25 *Event-driven exclusive gateway used as a start event.*

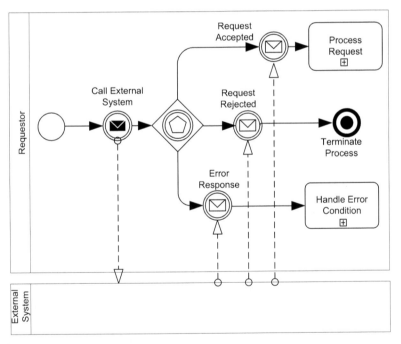

Figure 3.26 *Event-driven gateway used as an intermediate event.*

Processes use different data types to start the same process. In the example illustrated in Figure 3.26, the external system responds with one of three different messages. Because the message format is different for each condition, three different message types can be received. This pattern uses a single message event, followed by an exclusive gateway. In many scenarios, different message types arrive from other participants and require mapping to the needed message types.

This process pattern is useful when there are multiple suppliers or partner organizations (external participants). Often, the external participant has varying degrees of system automation capabilities. Some external participants might support a web services interaction, while others support file uploads. Still others need support for a manual process. Each method of receiving input needs different incoming message processing. Therefore, the event-based exclusive gateway is an excellent choice for diagramming this pattern.

The event-based gateway can use a message task instead of a message event. This notation can be used with other events, such as a timer.

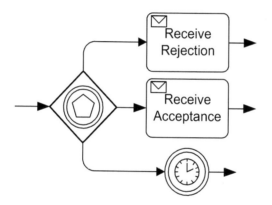

Figure 3.27 *Event-based gateway with message task and timer event.*

Figure 3.27 shows an example of message tasks used with a timer event. The process will either receive a rejection letter, an acceptance letter, or after the specified time has passed, the process will continue without either message.

Event-Based Parallel Gateway

A process might require receipt of multiple events before proceeding. This is the purpose of the parallel version of the event-driven gateway, the *event-driven parallel gateway*. Its shape is a combination gateway and parallel event, and it inherits the characteristics of both elements. Start or intermediate forms are inside a diamond.

The pattern for the parallel event-driven gateway includes a parallel gateway for the merge. Alone, the event-driven gateway is never used for a merge. Instead,

Figure 3.28 *Event-based inclusive gateway (parallel, start).*

Figure 3.29 *Event-based inclusive gateway (parallel, intermediate).*

a standard parallel gateway is used. It is a best practice to always include the parallel merge immediately following the connected events.

Figure 3.30 shows that more than one message is to be received, and a condition event is satisfied. If any of the events are not yet triggered, the process will not proceed. For example, the pattern could include an approval process with mandatory responses from two reviewers, as well as a business day constraint on the activity. When the second message was received on a weekend, the business day condition would not be true until Monday morning. Then it would trigger the condition, causing the process to continue.

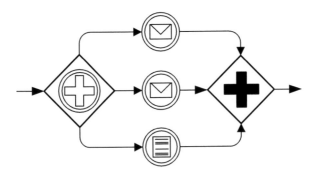

Figure 3.30 *Usage pattern for the event-based inclusive gateway.*

When used in an intermediate context, there is little difference between an event-driven parallel gateway and a standard parallel gateway. However, an event-based gateway models a process that does not start or continue until all the events are received. The ordinary parallel gateway signifies that the process has already begun and must now wait for the events. An instance of the process would not emerge until all the events occur. With a parallel gateway, the process instance will be running.

The intermediate version of the parallel event-based gateway can be used for documentation and to limit the scope of the subsequent flow to include events. Importantly, processes change over time, and BPMN includes several ways of expressing the exact process behavior.

Figure 3.31 shows a pattern that starts a service order process. This particular process begins in a unique way. Both a purchase order and a signed statement of work are required before the process can start (messages received). Additionally, the account must be in good standing (a condition). If all three of these conditions are not met, the process will not start.

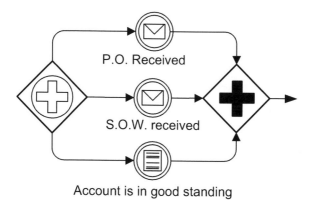

P.O. Received

S.O.W. received

Account is in good standing

Figure 3.31 *Parallel event-driven gateway as a start event.*

Without the event-driven parallel gateway, the example in Figure 3.31 would be more complicated to depict in BPMN. It is not known before the process starts which message will be received first. It is also not known whether or not the account is in good standing, which might change before or after either of the messages is received.

BPMN SCENARIOS

This section will review a number of BPMN examples that use what has already been covered in this chapter.

Coordinating Looping Processes

A common looping pattern in process modeling is to use a coordinator participant that makes decisions and dispatches requests to the proper role. The coordinator participant is a valuable abstraction. It can coordinate decisions for an entire organization. The coordinator is a participant that is aware of all activity. It decides and coordinates events across all other participants. Usually, a coordinator does not perform any of the tasks. Instead, the coordinator applies rules and dispatches tasks to other participants to complete. Figure 3.32 demonstrates a looping subprocess with a coordinator participant pool.

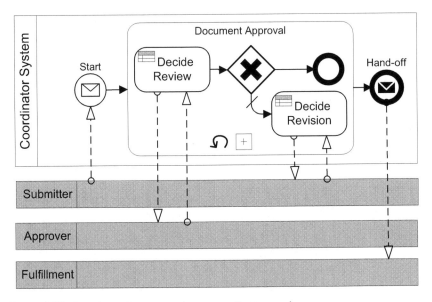

Figure 3.32 *Looping subprocess using a coordinator pool.*

Figure 3.32 is yet another pattern where decisions can direct processes. In this case, the decisions use the data in the request to select the participant—and probably the procedure—to be executed.

Figure 3.32 shows the participants involved in the process in a public process notation, and it also details how the participants interact. Figure 3.32 does not show the means of communication. For some process models, the interaction details might be important for synchronization purposes. For example, it might be important to show that a document approver is a person who is not normally involved in the full process. The approver must be alerted to do something. An alert implies an event, and a message interaction is the appropriate method of triggering an alerted action.

Figure 3.32 provides a decision-driven process model and is simpler to create. When the decisions coordinator is designed first, as in Figure 3.32, the overall design is faster and more complete. Additional participants are filled in after the decisions are modeled and process objectives have been properly diagrammed. The focus should be on process decisions first, rather than participants (swimlanes). This is because an analyst who draws a swimlane (pool or lane) might assign activity to a participant. In contrast, an analyst who models the decisions first will carefully consider the inclusion of each participant, as necessary, to support the process goals and objectives.

When used with different pools, the multiple-instance subprocess has some unique capabilities. The pattern shown in Figure 3.33 shows a voting process. First, a request is made for a vote from committee members. For each committee member, a vote request will be sent, and the process cannot continue until all members have voted.

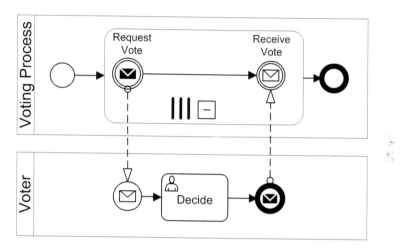

Figure 3.33 *Multiple-instance subprocess interaction.*

The messaging pattern shown in Figure 3.33 is often called asynchronous, meaning that a request will be sent, and separately, a reply will be made on another event. In contrast, Figure 3.34 shows a synchronous pattern which requires the process to wait for a reply before doing anything else. With asynchronous communication, the participant can do other activities between Request Vote and Receive Vote.

The parallel multiple-instance subprocess pattern in Figure 3.33 is common and particularly useful. Depicting this process behavior with a looping subprocess adds more complexity. First, a number of requests must be sent, and then later another subprocess that receives the same number of replies is sent. Figure 3.34 shows a looping subprocess pattern solution.

Because the looping subprocess is sequential, it can only interact with a single voter. By detaching the sending subprocess from the Receive Replies subprocess, Figure 3.34 mimics a parallel solution. This adds complexity for both the reviewer and the implementer.

The pattern in Figure 3.33 is simpler and better coordinates the voter response. In Figure 3.34, if a voter replies before all requests are sent, the reply would be lost. Because each instance of the subprocess is running independently,

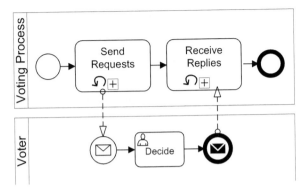

Figure 3.34 *Voting process with looping subprocesses.*

in parallel, the parallel multiple-instance in Figure 3.33 fixes this problem. Here, the send and receive can easily be managed within a single scope and clearly correlated.

DECISION LOGIC

There is tremendous value to a complete or even partial decision requirements diagram. The decomposition of decision making, the linking of required input data, and the identification of knowledge sources all clarify the exact nature of a decision in a business process. What they do not do is define the actual decision making logic that must be executed to make the decision.

DMN allows for a decision requirements diagram to be enhanced or extended with decision logic, optionally all the way to a completely executable specification of the decision making. To this end, decision logic can be specified for any decision or business knowledge model in a decision model. When adding decision logic to a decision requirements diagram, it is often not necessary to add any objects to the diagram; all the decision logic may be directly associated with the decisions already in the diagram. As the decision logic is specified, however, it may become clear that additional decomposition of the decision making or additional reusable business knowledge models make sense and should be added.

Decision Logic Representation

The decision logic required can be represented in three main ways in DMN:

- Literal expressions, which is text that describes how to derive a decision's result from its inputs.
- Decision tables which are tabular representations of decision logic, sometimes also known as rule sheets.

- Invocations which are demonstrated below in an invocation of a business knowledge model.

Literal expressions are the most flexible and can be purely descriptive text, such as a natural language description. More executable formats can include formal logic, a programming language such as Java, or rule syntax supported by a BRMS and Friendly Enough Expression Language (FEEL), which is part of DMN and described further in Chapter 4. Literal expressions could also be based on other standards such as Predictive Model Markup Language (PMML), which would allow the decision making logic to be defined in terms of an analytical model.

Decision tables are a very popular representation format for business rules and decision logic, and DMN supports a number of different layouts and approaches, described below.

The specification of an invocation allows a decision to be linked to a single business knowledge model so that the decision can invoke, or call, the decision logic defined in the business knowledge model, therefore reusing the decision logic specified in the business knowledge model.

Literal expressions can also include invocations of one or more business knowledge models. If there is decision logic required that is not in the invoked business knowledge model, or if there is more than one business knowledge model to be invoked for a specific decision, then a modeled invocation cannot be used, and a literal expression must be written that contains the invocation(s), as well as the additional logic.

Whatever the format, the decision logic consumes variables that represent the information requirements of the decision; each requirement has a variable that represents it. For literal expressions and decision tables, these requirements are mapped directly into the logic, while an invocation maps these to the variables defined for the business knowledge model.

Finally, the output of a decision's expression can be returned to a process model so that the action or actions suggested by the decision can be carried out. For instance, if the logic of a decision model decides that a particular offer is to be made to a customer, then the process can use the output of the decision to retrieve and actually present the offer to the customer.

Decision Tables

Three types of decision tables are defined in DMN:

1. Cross-tab or classic decision tables have dimensions that represent input variables, with each row and column in the table representing a specific condition based on the relevant input variable. Selecting a row and column based on specific values for those variables identifies a single cell

in the table. This cell contains the value to be assigned to the output of
the table.

Insurance Coverage Requirement						
Hazardous Material			Transportation Mode			
			Truck	Rail	Barge	Package
HAZMAT Product Category	1		$1M	$4M	$6M	$500K
	2		$6M		$4M	$100K
	3		$8M		$12M	$500K

Figure 3.35 *A cross-tab decision table.*

2. Decision tables with rules as rows. These decision tables are sometimes
    known as rule sheets, and in Figure 3.36, each column represents an
    input variable or an output variable. Each row contains values in zero,
    one or many of the input variable columns, as well as in one or more of
    the output columns. If the values in the input variables match all the
    columns in a row, then the rule is true, and that selects the appropriate
    output value(s).

Insurance Coverage Requirement			
UC	Hazardous Material Category	Transportation Mode	Coverage
	Class 1	Truck	$1M
		Rail	$4M
		Barge	$6M
		Package	$500K
	Class 2	Truck	$6M
		Rail	$6M
		Barge	$4M
		Package	$100K
	Class 3	Truck	$8M
		Rail	$8M
		Barge	$12M
		Package	$500K

Figure 3.36 *Rules as rows decision table.*

3. Decision table with rules as columns. These decision tables are also
    sometimes known as rule sheets and are a transposition of the rules as
    rows type. Each row is a variable, and each column is a rule.

Marketing Offer Selection			
Product	Product 1		Product 2
Offer Value	Low	High	
Marketing Offer	Offer A	Offer C	Offer B
UC	1	2	3

Figure 3.37 *Rules as columns decision table.*

It should be noted that compound outputs are allowed because each rule can set more than one output value, and the syntax allows merged cells as shown in Figure 3.35 for ease of reading.

Decision tables can be single or multiple hit tables. In a single hit table, only one result is allowed, while in a multiple hit table, many hits are allowed and more than one rule may be acted on. While DMN defines a number of hit policies and insists that these are displayed as part of the table, the core decision table hit policies that generally analysts should be restricted to are:

- Unique single hit tables where it is only ever possible for a single rule to be true, as the rules involved are exclusive.
- Any single hit tables where there may be many rules that are true at the same time, but it does not matter as they all result in the same output (e.g., a lot of ways to reject something).
- Multiple hit tables aggregate their results and valid use cases include those that collect all the hits to, for example, build a list of all the reasons for a rejection, as well as those that sum up a score based on all the rules that fire.

Other options for decision table hit policies are discussed in Chapter 4.

Business Knowledge Models

Business knowledge models act as functions, allowing decision logic to be parameterized and reused across decisions. For example, the decision logic for checking that a US address is valid may need to be applied in a decision that has an invoice as input data, as well as in a decision that has a purchase order as input data. If the logic is defined as a business knowledge model, then it can be reused across the two decisions.

Business knowledge models are linked to the decisions that use them for logic and to other business knowledge models that call them using knowledge requirements. They can also be linked, using authority requirements, to knowledge sources that describe where the logic originated.

Business knowledge models can be any decision logic: a decision table or a literal expression that contains business rules in a decision tree, rules in some other format, or non-rule formats such as predictive analytic models. Business knowledge models have parameters defined that are used in the decision logic and return a value or a business object containing values.

When a business knowledge model is invoked, whether using a modeled invocation or in a literal expression, the input values to the decision or business knowledge model doing the invoking are mapped to the business knowledge model's parameters, and the result of the business knowledge model is mapped to the output data. As implied in the example in Figure 3.1, when a decision is to be integrated in a process, these output data can drive conditions in gateways and values in activities.

While the decision logic for a decision requirements diagram may be added entirely to the decisions in the diagram, it is possible that some number of business knowledge models will be added either because the logic is reused (or intended to be reusable) or to provide easier management of certain pieces of business logic.

BPMN AND DMN DOCUMENTATION

Modelers can add information to DMN and BPMN diagrams to create clarity and improve understanding. BPMN has several inherent elements, artifacts, and data items for documentation. There is no equivalent in DMN for these; however, the tacit understanding of the specification writers was that things like the text box would be available in DMN.

Documentation in DMN is more abstract and a matter of using the metadata properly.

BPMN Documentation

BPMN provides the capability to append additional information to diagrams through shapes and annotations. There are three diagram documenting shapes: text annotation, associations, and groups. The shapes can be associated with other shapes but do not have a sequence flow or message flow. The dotted association line is used to attach text and data shapes to other BPMN shapes. Association lines attached to a data object may have an open arrowhead to indicate input or output data for an activity.

Because they can provide more written context about an activity than the activity name, text annotations are useful.

Text Annotation with more
details about an activity

Activities, events, and gateways will normally have a short label. One goal of creating a BPMN diagram is to provide clarity with good descriptions. A good

BPMN diagram is also concise and can be improved with text annotations and well-formed BPMN labels.

While DMN does not include a similar text annotation approach today, it is likely to do so in the future. This kind of annotation can provide benefits to DMN models also and should be used as necessary to improve readability and understanding.

Groups

The group shape denotes a common purpose to a group of shapes. The group shape is drawn as a rounded corner rectangle with a dot-dash-dot-dash pattern, as shown here.

The group shape is permitted on the process diagram above pools and lanes. A group shape surrounds other shapes located anywhere in the diagram. The group illustrates related activities, even when they cross multiple participants (see Figure 3.38). As a non-executing alternative to a subprocess, the group shape might surround shapes inside the pool.

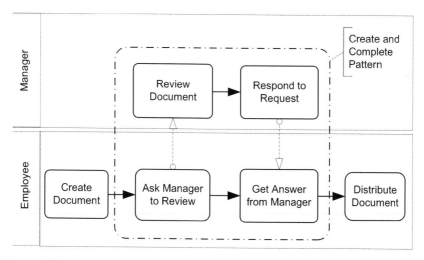

Figure 3.38 *The group shape encircles related activities in two participant pools.*

DMN does not include a group shape, but there is real value to being able to draw groups on DMN diagrams. Sets of decisions and business knowledge models might be grouped to show implementation boundaries or project phases, for example, while groups of input data might show which information objects are delivered to the system together.

Data Object

The data object can be used as a means to document a diagram and a mechanism for connecting a schema to a BPMN model. The data object is a rectangle with the upper right corner folded over, as shown here:

Purchase Order

The text label for a data object is underneath the shape. Often, the current state of the data object is shown as an attribute placed in brackets under the text label. As the diagram progresses, the state of the data object can easily be read, as illustrated in Figure 3.39.

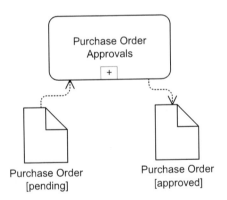

Figure 3.39 *Use of data shapes.*

As with the text annotation, the association line connects the data to another shape. Data shapes are often associated with tasks, gateways, events, sequence lines, or message lines. In message flow, data objects portray the payload or content of messages.

The central purpose of the data object is to add the details necessary to make a process model executable. Data objects also add more information about the behavior of the execution process. More details about data objects will be covered in the chapter on execution semantics.

In DMN, there is a formal object for data: the input data shape. It is extremely useful if the data objects in process models have a matching input data representation in related decision models. See also Information Items below.

DMN Documentation

There are no explicit graphical elements for documenting DMN. However, there are additional properties and associations worth tracking for DMN objects. These are defined in DMN as metadata properties of the various objects, but no specific notation is given for them. The power of questions and allowed answers has been discussed in defining decisions, as well as the importance of tracking which processes and tasks used a particular decision. The relationship of decisions to objectives, organizations, and other context also matter.

Objectives and Metrics

DMN allows for OMG's Business Motivation Model (BMM)[1] objectives and KPIs or metrics to be linked to the decisions that impact them. This mapping can be used to put each decision, or at least the top-level decisions that are not required by other decisions, into a business context. This involves assessing the KPIs and objectives in the business area and determining which KPIs or objectives are impacted by each decision. A decision impacts a KPI or objective if changing the way the decision is made could be reasonably expected to have an impact on the value recorded for the KPI or objective.

The BMM describes a way of documenting how objectives are achieved. An instance of a decision can be associated with multiple supported objectives and performance indicators.

Organizational Impact

Decision making is central to organizations, and the various roles played in decision making by an organization matters. Three particular roles can be played by organizations, organizational units, or roles, like those in BMM. For repeatable decisions, these relationships are not generally to an individual but to a team, department, or role within a team or department. It should also be noted that multiple organizations or roles can own, make, or care about a specific decision. DMN defines two such roles:

- **Who owns the decision?** Who decides how the decision should be made? Who is the approver of the approach taken? Who decides that we shall

---

1.   Object Management Group, Inc.: Business Motivation Model, http://www.omg.org/spec/BMM/1.2/

decide this way and not that way? Who will be maintaining the business rules for this decision?

- **Who makes the decision?** Often, one part or level of the organization owns a decision, but a different part or level makes the day-to-day decisions. Sales management might own the pricing decision, for example, but pricing decisions are made by the sales teams themselves. If decisions are automated or partially automated, then the organization that passes on the decision to a customer or supplier could be considered the decision maker as well.

It is often also worth documenting other stakeholders in the decision. While many decisions have owners and makers, other parts of the organization might have a stake or interest and expect their opinions to be taken into account.

Other Context

In addition to a decision's relationship to business processes and the tasks that invoke them, consider tracking the relationships of decisions to objects such as business events or information systems.

Information Items

Input data objects, the output of decisions, and the parameters and output of business knowledge models can be formally defined in DMN using information items. Information items are a basic hierarchical information structure such that each can be a single data item, a structure of other data items, or a collection of either of these. A basic set of DMN types can be used, or external types can be referenced. Restrictions on the allowed values can be specified using expressions.

When a DMN model is extended to the point of complete specification, using FEEL for example (see Chapter 4), the information manipulated by the decisions, business knowledge models, and decision logic must be fully specified. In other circumstances, some degree of documentation of the information items will be required to show what information is being used where.

COMBINING SIGNALS AND OTHER EVENTS

As the capabilities of BPMN are beginning to be visualized, more complex or subtle situations can be modeled.

Figure 3.40 shows a busy intersection from the perspective of three participants: a northbound driver, a westbound driver, and the traffic light that helps the two drivers avoid a collision. Drivers entering the intersection determine whether or not to proceed based on the color of the traffic light. The driver observes the state and decides. Because the traffic light occurs during normal driving, the traffic signal light is a driver's signal event. The stopped driver proceeds through the intersection if there is a green signal. From the perspective of the traffic light, a green signal is send to traffic waiting at a red light through the intersection.

Without participants, there is no explicit message interaction. Instead of using interaction lines, Figure 3.40 uses the group shape to clarify the relationship between the signal throw and catch events. The usage of the group shape is a documentation notation; it makes the diagram easier to read.

Figure 3.40 illustrates what happens after the signal change. The northbound driver is reckless and hits the accelerator pedal. The westbound driver is more cautious and watches for crossing traffic even though the traffic light signals green. When a speeding driver crosses with indifference to the red signal, an error handling subprocess is managed with this exception condition.

This is an example of how easy it is to represent a complex interaction using just a few BPMN shapes. In fact, if the whole scenario was written in words, there would probably be three or four pages. This succinct diagram shows the perspective of three participants, what they do, and how each action relates to the other participants.

The process in Figure 3.40 contrasts the condition and signal events. In the event gateway in the condition event shape, participants actively monitor for a condition. There is no guarantee that a signal light will be encountered while driving (the condition). The default event is the green condition, where the criterion is that the signal is recognized, observed, relevant to the driver's lane, and currently green. Otherwise the driver waits for a red signal to turn green (a broadcast).

With the signal event shape, participants observe a broadcast message. The driver subscribes to the signal event and waits for it. The signal event is received by anyone within view of the traffic light (the subscribers). The signal is used in this case because there is already a potential participant. In contrast, the condition event is used when it is not known if a related process exists or not. This is because the act of locating a traffic signal and responding to its current state is fairly complex. It requires a driver to pay attention to many objects as he drives down the road. If the traffic signal were instead an ambulance siren, a signal would be a better choice. With complex criteria for event recognition, a condition should be used instead of a signal.

Figure 3.41 shows a process where the sales team needs a contract reviewed by the legal team. The contract is not directly created by the sales team. Instead, the contract is generated by a system. First, the CRM data source is updated. Some additional information might be retrieved from the CRM system that automatically populates the contract documents. Contracts are generated, and the legal team is notified with a hyperlink that points to the document location on a network file share.

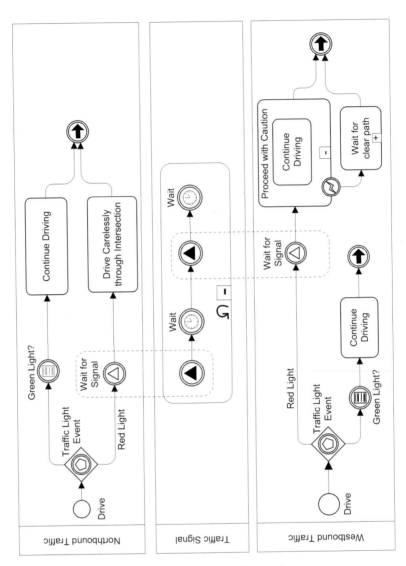

Figure 3.40 *Traffic light diagram using the signal event shapes.*

SUMMARY

This chapter covered several useful event types in BPMN. Modelers can develop fairly complete processes with the information in this (and the previous two) chapters. This chapter also covered some of the more powerful shapes in BPMN. These shapes are composites of the behaviors and notations described in the first BPMN chapter.

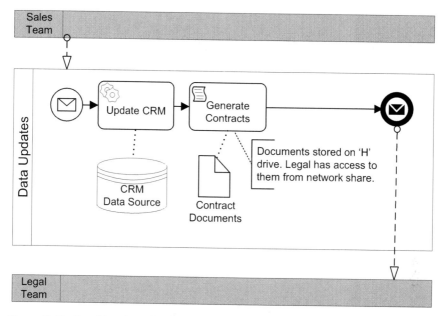

Figure 3.41 *Combination of multiple document shapes and annotations.*

The chapter also covered six additional tasks that are denoted with special markers. These were:

- Manual task (hand marker): A manual activity outside the scope of a BPMS.
- Human task (person marker): A task performed by a person, used to differentiate people and system tasks.
- Message task (envelope marker): A task involving interaction with another participant.
- Service task (gear marker): A task performed by a system service.
- Script task (script marker): A software script that runs automatically.
- Rule task (table marker): An activity run by business rules, often linked to DMN decision models.

Next, this chapter covered timer events and introduced the non-interrupting timer event. This provided a strong foundation for learning about events that are attached to the boundaries of subprocesses.

Next, the signal event was described.

Looping activities provide important capabilities for processing sets of records or executing until a condition is met.

BPMN provides the link event to simplify large diagrams. There are two types of link events, intermediate catching and throwing.

The event-based gateway solves a common, yet complex scenario. When a process should start upon the receipt of multiple starting messages with different data types, it should use the event-driven gateway with intermediate events.

These shapes address an important situation: multiple events that start or participate in a process. They are composites of the basic elements of gateways and events. In order to model more complex business processes, these are necessary knowledge. The next chapter will complete the tools needed to manage events.

This chapter also set out the logic elements of a decision model, especially the decision table. Logic elements can be combined into decision requirements diagrams to describe precisely how a decision can be executed. That is, diagrams can be extended with decision logic to form a complete definition of exactly how the user wishes to make a decision.

One purpose of using BPMN and DMN is to reduce text documentation that describes a complex process or decision. To accomplish this, as many details as necessary must be included to illustrate the intent of the model.

CHAPTER 4

HANDLING COMPLEXITY

Previously, this book described the core building blocks that make up process flow in BPMN and decisions in DMN. This chapter builds on these concepts. When used with the shapes and patterns introduced in this chapter, BPMN can model processes with increasing complexity. DMN supports complex models without additional shapes or constructs; it provides detailed logic capabilities. The use of DMN to model decisions within a process also helps handle complexity by ensuring that decision making complexity is in a separately managed decision model and not forced into a process model.

In Chapter 2, the BPMN shapes focused on supported "happy path" modeling and left the harder work of cleaning up the messes of errors or special conditions for this chapter. For the most part, the BPMN in Chapters 2 and 3 never leave the "guard rails" of sequences and messages. Yet processes still can fail for business and technical reasons, and it can be useful to jump out of the process and manage or try to recover. This is the exceptional condition path. Interestingly, with non-interrupting events, business exceptions can be managed without stopping the ongoing instance.

In addition to happy path BPMN modeling, there are atypical modeling scenarios managed by the complex gateway and, arguably, the signal event.

Handling errors and exceptions is critical for building robust processes. This chapter presents a number of common patterns that will simplify modeling efforts.

With respect to DMN, Chapter 2 discussed the basic elements—decisions knowledge sources, input data, and business knowledge—and showed how these can be related using different kinds of requirements. DMN elements and their requirements can be diagrammed on one or more decision requirement diagrams to build a decision model or a decision requirements model. Within this model, the decision logic of individual decisions and business knowledge models can be specified using decision tables.

Chapter 3 introduced the basics of expressing the underlying decision logic—the business rules—of a decision model. The specifics of expressions used in these decision tables and elsewhere in a fully specified decision model are discussed in this chapter. In addition, more advanced decision requirement modeling issues are considered. Finally, this chapter includes some notes on more complex interactions between decision models and process models.

COMPLEX GATEWAY

Thus far, this book has reviewed five different gateways. Each of these gateways produces and consumes a specified number of tokens. The exclusive gateways (data-based and multiple) create a flow of a single token. The parallel and inclusive gateways (parallel, data-based, and multiple parallel) create a flow of multiple tokens. Sometimes a process scenario requires a more dynamic management of the merging tokens. For example, imagine that four different activities seek an answer or result, and either two or three of them produce the answer. Here, the modeler will need to compute the result. Completion of the gateway sequence is based on the number of tokens that arrive or on the number that need to be produced. For this, BPMN provides the complex gateway. The complex gateway is a diamond shape with an enclosed asterisk, as shown here.

This gateway configures a series of parallel paths, either splitting or merging. It also handles a complex problem: the need to cancel execution of one or more arises out of the execution of another. This is known as *dead path elimination*. Complex gateways can set conditions on incoming tokes and enable a process to synchronize fewer paths from the total number of incoming transitions. With the complex gateway, parallel (or inclusive) branches converge, and outbound activity is activated once the incoming branches are complete. The result of the remaining branches is ignored. Execution of the complex merge is blocked until all of the incoming branches have been completed.

Complex Split

A use case to declare an executive review of a product line requires a business process to check concurrently whether the product has high legal liabilities, is subject to frequent quality post-manufacture returns, and has unsatisfactory internal quality checks. The outcomes of these checks is to be evaluated so that as soon as two of these checks pass and the product doesn't have any high liabilities, a clean product state is declared and the third check is aborted.

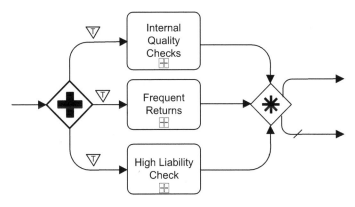

Figure 4.1 *An example of the use of a complex gateway.*

The three steps are run in parallel as threaded by the parallel split. Three tokens are generated and must be consumed somehow. The outcome of responses coming from each of the subprocesses is evaluated by the complex gateway. This is an example of a two of three join with one mandatory condition to be met. According to the execution semantics, if the Frequent Returns subprocess and the High Liability Check subprocess passes, then the Internal Quality Checks would be cancelled, and the instance associated with the subprocess is cancelled.

Complex gateways can be used to explicitly skip activities. This might be simple to denote as a business rule because, in essence, a decision is being made concerning the next steps to be taken. In addition, the behavior of the complex gateway is complicated to understand from a visual examination. Moreover, using OR gates that negate the sequences are also hard to understand. The complex gateway introduces a "reset output" to abort all pending flows and create a token on the optional reset output flow. This is a very powerful yet subtle semantic.

Arguably, complex gateways are difficult to understand, and unless dynamic rules are needed about the number of tokens that are generated in the split and con-sumed in the merge, complex gateways are generally not needed and can be replaced with a decision flow.

Complex Merge

A process model might have a number of gateway paths that include a composite of exclusive, inclusive, and parallel transitions. These can be merged with the complex gateway merge.

If the conditions for merging are not dynamic, and there is no need to cancel an activity as in the dead path elimination, then a complex gateway is probably not needed. Consider the diagram in Figure 4.2 where a complex merge is used.

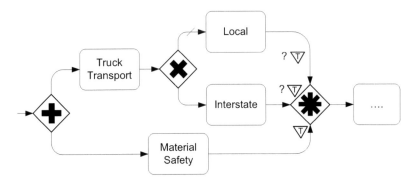

Figure 4.2 *Questionable usage of the complex merge gateway.*

The complex merge gateway shown in Figure 4.2 is used for the same pattern in Figures 4.3 and 4.4; however, the gateway needs to be configured to decide the activation count. In the activation count, the number of tokens that must arrive to activate the gateway must be set. All the logic from a complex merge shape can be defined in a subprocess (Figure 4.3). Without the subprocess, explicit merges should be used (Figure 4.4).

Because subprocesses have an implicit parallel split and merge, the subprocess might be able to solve some complex merge challenges. Only the complex split should be used and merged when there is a dead path elimination requirement. Instead, the subprocess can accomplish the diagram's objective. As noted earlier, the use of a decision making task can cleanly handle some of these complex situations.

The patterns in Figure 4.3 and 4.4 are somewhat equivalent. Figure 4.4 is more compact and uses a subprocess implicit split-and-merge pattern. Even without the complex merge, a subprocess might be suggested in Figure 4.3. To improve clarity in Figure 4.4, a parallel gateway before the "Truck Transport" and "Material Safety" activities can be considered, and the rest can be left unchanged. Either way, the meaning stays the same. With this thinking, it can be easy to find implicit split-and-merge patterns in the subprocesses. Outside a subprocess, use explicit splits and merges.

EVENTS AND ERROR HANDLING

For the most past, the BPMN modeling discussed in this book has been confined to the happy path or to process flows that stay on the guard rails of sequences and

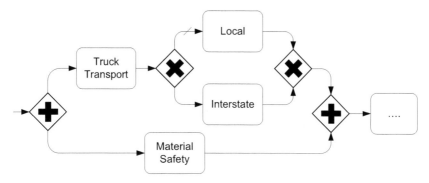

Figure 4.3 *A complex merge pattern solved with explicit merge points.*

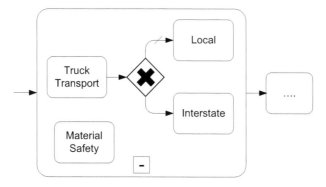

Figure 4.4 *A complex merge pattern using a subprocess.*

messages. However, it is important to consider what happens when the flow needs to jump away from the norm and handle exceptional situations.

Integrating an error processing strategy into the process can be challenging. Fortunately, BPMN provides powerful approaches to managing failures in the form of event subprocesses, exceptions, and escalations. The patterns covered here will create processes that are survivable and hardened. The exception and escalation shapes allow continuous operation throughout intermittent error conditions, such as those encountered in integrating cloud services and resources. Without a hardened process, participants might need to use a manual process for the exception flow. Manual processes promote staff improvisations and undocumented work-around—and obviously should be avoided.

Event Subprocess

Event subprocesses were a major change to the BPMN specification and created a slightly different, albeit intuitive, appearance. The event subprocess is characterized by an event followed by a sequence of tasks and events.

The event subprocess is a specialized subprocess that is used within a process (or subprocess). A subprocess is started when the first event in the sequence is triggered. As shown in Figure 4.5 below, that event can be interrupting, as in a solid-line circle, or non-interrupting, as with the dotted-line circle. Event subprocesses are located within processes or subprocess and are called out by dotted-line frames. The specification also allows the dotted line to be collapsed with the [+] notation.

The event subprocess type can only be used for interrupting or non-interrupting catching events. An event subprocess starts with a catching start error event. In contrast, events on a subprocess border serve the same purpose but always catch with an intermediate event.

Figure 4.5 *A simple event subprocess that reports data to a state without interrupting the central process.*

In Figure 4.5, the main process could have a gateway that checks for the need to notify the state and raises a non-interrupting event sub process.

This is the second place where a variation on the usage of the non-interrupting event is encountered. With this, the event subprocess can execute a sequence of activities without interrupting the central process, and it uses a start event shape. For instance, a special report must be completed for shipments that travel through a particular state. In 4.1, the event subprocess can be triggered as non-interrupting and create the report. The advantage to this approach is that these routines, such as report handling routines, can be standardized as a call subprocess.

Error and Escalation Events

The error and escalation events are similar in that they provide a way to stop an ongoing subprocess and change the course or correct a situation. Further, an escalation event can also throw events and continue processing without stopping the process or subprocess. The difference is that error events always stop the branch of the subprocess that they are on. Errors do not cancel other active tokens. If there are ongoing sequences or activities in parallel, these must be handled, or additional errors will be generated.

The error event shapes either generate an error code to be raised, or catch and handle an error condition. When an error condition is raised, it is thrown. Next, the error condition is caught by another shape, or it is escalated to a level that can catch the error. Depending on the circumstances, an error that is not trapped can crash the process.

The error event shapes include the intermediate error event and the error end event. Similar to the message intermediate events, there are two variations of the error intermediate event: the unfilled (white) icon for the catching version and the filled (black) icon for the throwing version. The start, intermediate, catching, and ending error events are displayed as shown here:

Event Type	BPMN	Used
Start Error Event (catching)		In event subprocesses
Intermediate Error Event (catching)		On process boundaries
End Error Event		At the end of sequences

Escalations represent a planned condition created inside the process that must be handled outside the normal flow. An escalation event denotes that, while performing a task, this escalation can be issued and trigger the actions specified in the diagram. The current process or task can be cancelled, or other activity flow can take place in parallel (non-interrupting). An escalation denotes a more ad hoc or looser process flow.

Similar to the error intermediate events, there are three variations of the escalation intermediate event: the unfilled (white) icon for the catching version and the filled (black) icon for the throwing version. There is also a non-interrupting variation. The shapes and the places used are shown here:

Event Type	BPMN	Uses
Start Escalation Event (catching)		Event subprocess
Non-Interrupting Start Escalation Event (catching)		Event subprocess
Intermediate Escalation Event (catching)		Subprocess or process boundary
Non-Interrupting Escalation Event (catching)		Subprocess boundary
Intermediate Escalation Event (throwing)		Process sequences
End Escalation Event		Process sequences

Like the timer event, error and escalation events can be connected to a sub-process or to a transition.

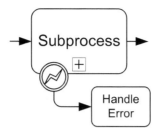

Figure 4.6 *Basic exception handling flow.*

Modeling Error Handling
Three Error Types

There are three types of exceptions that may affect process execution:

1. Technical exceptions: The process server has failed.
2. Transient exceptions: A needed resource (e.g, a cloud service) for the process is unavailable, perhaps temporarily.
3. Business exceptions: The condition of the process is in error. Data is incomplete or has errors.

Unfortunately, there is no cure or notation for the technical exception. When the server halts, recovering processes are dependent on the technical nature of the process server.

Decisions can create named business exceptions. Generally, the exceptions are going to be responses or answers like any other. These can then be handled using the appropriate BPMN elements and may result in the generation of a formal error in BPMN as shown in Figure 4.7. If the process is transactional, it should compensate for transactions that fail to complete. In compensation, the process cleans up or backs out records from ERP systems, operational data stores, or data warehouses.

Processes often must be completed within a specific time period, so there could be time-out actions noted on the diagram. Business processes usually receive a message and translate that message into yet another message for consumption by the next part of the process. BPMN is powerful for developing time-outs, exceptions, and compensations. In building a basic process in BPMN, time-outs, exceptions, and compensations can be attached directly to an event subprocess. When time-outs and exceptions occur within the process tasks, the process server traps these and launches the subprocess or moves to the boundary of the subprocess.

BPMN Patterns for Error Handling

The error and escalation shapes can be used to create the exceptional path, and this path might contain multiple steps that handle the error. The most basic pattern is to capture the error, process it, and rejoin the flow. Multiple steps must be grouped in the exceptional flow into a subprocess, as in Figure 4.7. In this example, the error was raised to the subprocess boundary, and two activities were needed to correct the error. The flow rejoins the process at the "Complete" task.

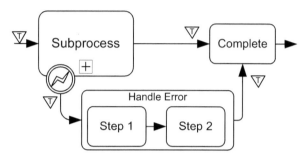

Figure 4.7 *Using subprocess for exceptional flow.*

Exceptional error flow is always interrupting: the subprocess that generated the error will terminate, and the alternate "exceptional flow" is followed. Next, the process can merge the exceptional flow with the main flow. The exceptional flow merge does not need to immediately return to the subprocess that generated the error. A process model can merge several steps downstream. When merging, it is important to consider what is happening with the tokens. Interrupting flow can use exclusive merge patterns— either implicit as shown in Figure 4.7, or with the addition of an exclusive gateway at the merge point, as shown in Figure 4.8.

Figure 4.8 shows an error event used at the boundary as created by a decision that looks at the validity of the data. Business rules in the decision will look at the attributes of the data and decide if the information is correct. The result of the decision will not only validate the data; it can tell the calling process how to correct or manage the error. It does this by setting attributes on the output data of the rule task. For example, an attribute might state that a budget number is over-allocated, and a notice can be generated to an account manager.

Decisions play an important role in error handling. Processes and users send data into a process in application servers. If they send incorrect data, as decided by DMN, then a business exception has occurred. The resulting process steps resolve the error.

When a token leaves a subprocess, activities outside the process do not have direct access to the subprocess' data. Therefore, any data generated in the subprocess might be lost if the error occurs before a save. To retain data in the event of an error, the modeler might use an event subprocess with a start error event. Again,

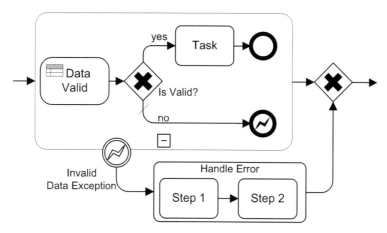

Figure 4.8 *Subprocess scopes and error handling decided by a decision and with explicit merge.*

Figure 4.9 also shows a start error event used in an event subprocess as created by a decision that looks at the validity of the data. The start error is only used for exceptional flow within an event subprocess.

Exceptional flow inside an event subprocess has access to the same data and conditions as its parent scope. Therefore, in Figure 4.9, any data created while executing tasks one or two would be accessible to the error handler. In contrast, steps one and two of the error handler in Figure 4.8 require special handling of the data. This will become a more important concept later as transactions are discussed.

Process models often specify error conditions with a pair, a throwing end error and a catching intermediate error connected to a subprocess. End error events, not handled in the scope of the subprocess or larger process, do not need this matching intermediate process.

Errors arise from a number of conditions. Web services and databases might be offline for longer periods than a service level required. Data from employees or trading partners might be incorrect. Errors can be detected in the process data through business rules or in combination with different events in the process. It is often necessary to define a number of errors for different conditions.

Error events throw variables that can be caught by subsequent intermediate errors. In a subprocess, different error handling procedures are needed for different conditions. Figure 4.10 shows a process with multiple error handlers for different conditions. One condition, the decision error, merges with the main sequence flow. The other error event handler causes a link event, which implies a loop back to the start of the subprocess.

There are a number of approaches to handling the exceptional path. When there are non-interrupting events involved, the exceptional flow must be merged.

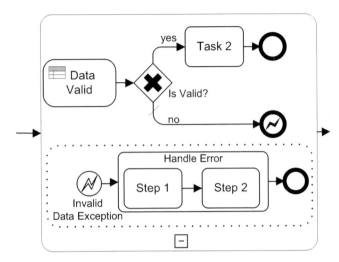

Figure 4.9 *Exception flow inside the subprocess with a start error event.*

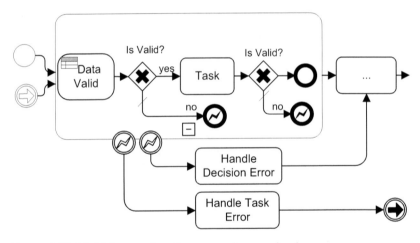

Figure 4.10 *Multiple error handlers on a subprocess border.*

Figure 4.11 shows an example of an explicit merge on an exclusive gateway after an interrupting event.

When non-interrupting events are introduced into the pattern, there are a number of ways to merge the paths. Because the scenario is non-interrupting, an additional token is generated, and tokens in the calling path continue. The non-interrupting exceptional flow need not merge with the normal flow; it can simply end. Because there are now multiple tokens, these paths merge in parallel. Figure 4.12 shows this pattern. Because not all paths are active, the parallel

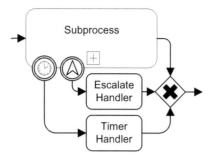

Figure 4.11 *Interrupting merge pattern.*

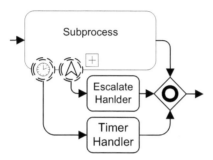

Figure 4.12 *Non-interrupting merge pattern.*

gateway would not handle the exception. The exclusive gateway would not work because more than one path could potentially be active.

Exception and escalation handling can combine interrupting and non-interrupting events on the same subprocess. Figure 4.13 shows this hybrid merge pattern.

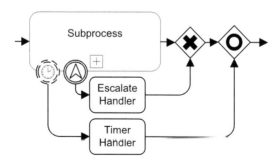

Figure 4.13 *Hybrid merge pattern.*

Figure 4.13 solves the problem of combining an interrupting and a non-interrupting event. But what if the interrupting escalation occurs after the non-interrupting timer? Should the timer handler continue? In Figure 4.13, the timer handler would continue until completed, regardless of the state of the escalation handler. This might suggest a complex merging condition; however, there is a better solution that incorporates the event subprocess.

Figure 4.14 shows a hybrid merge pattern using an event subprocess for the non-interrupting merge condition. The timer event is non-interrupting. Therefore, it can occur in parallel with the normal activity. The interrupting escalation condition is handled with a standard exclusive merge pattern, external from the subprocess. In this case, if escalation event is thrown from the activity enclosed in the subprocess, the entire parent subprocess cancels along with the potential timer event. Therefore, the timer, its corresponding event subprocess handler, and all activities are cancelled when escalation occurs. The escalation event has full override capacity, including any enclosed non-interrupting events and exceptional flows contained within the subprocess.

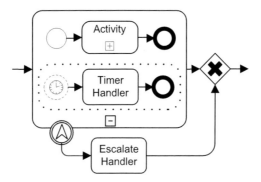

Figure 4.14 *Using a subprocess to solve merge challenges.*

The subprocess in Figure 4.15 is a hybrid of interrupting/non-interrupting events merging. Start events are used for the both exceptional condition handlers. The differences between the normal start, non-interrupting, and interrupting events are shown on this pattern.

The pattern in Figure 4.15 is nearly identical to that of Figure 4.14, with one small difference. Both event handlers are using an event subprocess contained within the parent subprocess. The escalation handler activity has access to the same data scope as the other activities contained in the top-level subprocess.

The modeling style in Figure 4.15 is most useful when an immediate merge is desired, and it is simpler to draw than Figure 4.14. However, processes cannot merge upstream in the process, as in Figure 4.16.

The escalation event handler in Figure 4.16 is designed to route an activity to someone else, possibly a manager. After the manager determines the course of action, the subprocess will reset back to its previous state. For example, the manager decides, then routes the activity back to the work queue for all customer ser-

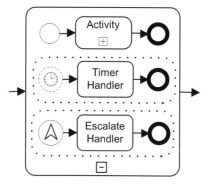

Figure 4.15 *Using start event as exceptional condition handlers.*

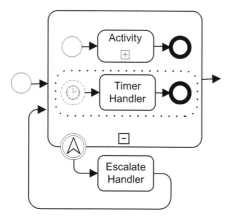

Figure 4.16 *Upstream flow with an event handler.*

vice agents. There should only be one instance of the enclosed activity occurring at any one time. To prevent the possibility of multiple instances in parallel, an interrupting border event handler is used. With the intermediate catching escalation event, the parent subprocess is cancelled, and a new one is created when the subprocess is restarted.

It is important to know what event can be used as non-interrupting. Tables 4.1 and 4.2 show what shapes can be used in each situation:

In subprocess interrupting, the shape can be used inside of a subprocess as an event handler. When used as event handlers, the sequence coming from the event is exceptional flow.

Not all start events have both interrupting and non-interrupting capability. For example, error and compensation events are always interrupting. Also note

Table 4.1 Start Event Usage

Start Events			
Event Type	**Process Sequences**	**Event Subprocess Interrupting**	**Event Subprocess Non-Interrupting**
Empty	?		
Message	?	?	?
Timer	?	?	?
Error		?	
Escalation		?	?
Cancel			
Compensation		?	
Condition	?	?	?
Signal	?	?	?
Multiple	?	?	?
Parallel Multiple	?	?	?

Table 4.2 Intermediate Event Usage

Intermediate Events				
Event Type	**Sequences Catching**	**Subprocess Boundary Interrupting**	**Subprocess Boundary Non-Interrupting**	**Sequences Throwing**
Empty	?			
Message	?	?	?	?
Timer	?	?	?	
Error		?		
Escalation		?	?	?
Cancel		?		
Compensation		?		?
Condition	?	?	?	
Link	?			?
Signal	?	?	?	?
Multiple	?	?	?	
Parallel Multiple	?	?	?	

that some events shapes do not have a start event, such as cancel, link, and terminate.

Subprocess boundary means that the shape can be attached to a subprocess border. It is important to note that not all shapes have both interrupting and non-interrupting capability. For example, error and compensation events are always interrupting.

Top-level throwing means that the intermediate shape can throw an event from within a sequence flow. Intermediate throwing signal, link, and message events are common in normal flow.

BPMN TRANSACTION HANDLING MECHANISM

Transactions have a special notation that differs from events and activities. Transactional subprocesses are denoted with a double-line border. Inside a transaction activity, special activities, called compensators, are used to "roll back" or reverse a previous action performed. The compensators can be triggered in two ways, either by explicitly throwing compensation event or implicitly by throwing a cancel event.

The double border also denotes that the process engine uses a transactional algorithm to the events. Usually this has ACID (atomicity, consistency, isolation, durability)[1] properties that guarantee that database transactions are processed reliably. The syntax of the following BPMN shapes details the steps of transactional assurance.

Compensation Events

There are four BPMN symbols for compensation events, as shown here.

Event Type	BPMN	Uses
Start Compensation Event		Event Subprocess
Intermediate Compensation Event?(catching)		Subprocess boundary

---

1. ACID (atomicity, consistency, isolation, durability) is a set of properties that guarantees database transactions are processed reliably.

Intermediate Compensation Event?(throwing)		Sequence
End Compensation Event		Sequence
Compensation Activity	Task	In transaction subprocesses

In addition to the events, there is a special activity type that is used for compensation handlers.

Some ACID activities create a specific output or a committing of data that may need reversal if it is determined that a transaction should not proceed. The compensation event and compensation handling activities are used for this scenario. Compensation events are not shown within the process flow. Instead, the sequences of compensation activities are shown with the association line. A compensation handler activity is an automatic activity that activates when a compensation event is thrown. A compensation handler activity can be a single task, or it can be a subprocess when multiple rollback steps are required for a transaction.

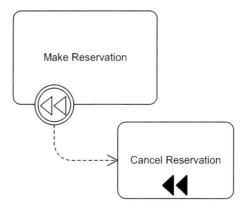

Figure 4.17 *Compensation intermediate event and an associated Compensation handler task.*

Processes often produce groups of transactions in databases or application services called nested transactions. A set or nesting of these transactions is called a *savepoint*. In rollbacks, transactions at a savepoint are removed. The compensation event shapes include the intermediate compensation event and the compensation end event. A pair of shapes specifies a compensation condition: an end compensation and an intermediate compensation connected to a subprocess.

Like the error event, a process cannot start with a compensation event; however, an event subprocess can start with a compensation event. Optionally, the compensation end event shape can indicate a distributed transaction rollback. Use of the end compensation event is an explicit way of causing compensation. Compensation events can also be implicit within the scope of a transaction. If a transaction were to fail, all compensation handlers within a transaction subprocess should automatically start the rollback steps associated with each activity inside the transaction.

BPMN treats each subprocess as a separate, long-running transaction. The transaction records all sequences of activities. Because transactions in a business process approach might require lengthy periods to complete, traditional mechanisms for saving database data are not always appropriate. As the process executes, data might be saved to one or more, or even many, databases. The idea of the long-running transaction relies on grouping these databases into smaller transaction sets. Therefore, the process must undo the partial results of a failed subprocess.

Compensation handlers reverse the effect of a finished unit of work in a business process. However, because a process is not aware of the details of a database transaction, the model must specify how the reversal happens. The process invokes the compensation when an error or unexpected condition arises during the normal work of the process. This cleans up the process for the compensation handler to start its reversal activity.

Cancel Events

There are two cancel events, the intermediate and end cancel event, as shown here.

The cancel events are used with a subprocess that processes a transaction. There are only two types, the cancel end event that throws the condition and the cancel intermediate event that catches the condition. The cancel intermediate event can only be placed on the border of a subprocess.

The cancel end event is used when a condition is discovered that does not require compensation but will cause the transaction to cancel. Figure 4.18 shows the proper usage of the cancel event shapes. When a user tries to update a database record that does not exist, the transaction is simply cancelled.

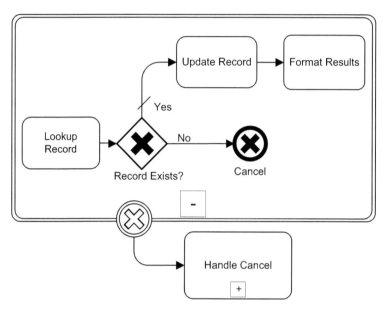

Figure 4.18 *The use of cancel events.*

The cancel event must be used properly and not confused with compensation events. Compensations back out transactions with reverse steps where data is partly written.

The cancel end event is similar to the terminate event. The cancel event, however, does not terminate the entire process, just the surrounding subprocess. If the model's objective is to stop all activities in the entire participant pool, the terminate event should be used instead.

Figure 4.19 shows the combined use of cancel and compensation. An activity inside the transaction subprocess requires compensation when the transaction fails or cancels. The end cancel event throws, and the intermediate cancel event on the subprocess border catches

The sequence flow from the intermediate cancel event leads to an exception flow that notifies the customer, then cancels the entire process with the terminate event. Because the compensation handler is inside a transaction subprocess, the compensation should automatically take place if the transaction is rolled back. A

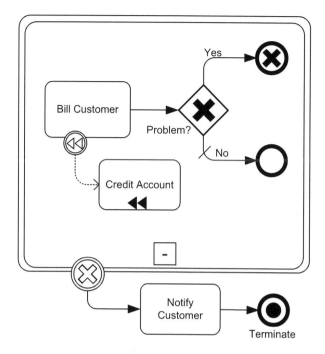

Figure 4.19 *Combined usage of cancel, compensation, and terminate events.*

compensation end event could be used in place of the cancel end event, but this only allows one activity to be associated with compensation. All other intermediate catching events allow for sequence flow.

COMPLEX SCENARIOS IN BPMN

A combination of event subprocesses and transactions can be used to precisely control a process and manage errors in a succinct way.

The following scenario revisits the importance of compensations. As an example, suppose the user wants to make tea. Tea cannot be made unless the user has tea bags or tea leaves, water, and a teapot. The user will not know if she has all three required items until she goes to retrieve them. If she does not have all the required items, then she must return the other items. Errors might occur in this scenario, such as the tea leaves being moldy (See Figure 4.20) The model either associates each activity with an inverse action when the transaction fails or uses a subprocess to handle all compensation in the handler activity. Either way, the association dotted line is used instead of the sequence flow solid line. Individual compensation handlers were used in this case because each activity required a specialized inverse activity to compensate for the transaction failure

Figure 4.20 shows two ways of triggering compensation. The missing ingredients error starts an exceptional flow, which triggers each compensation explicitly and separately. The stale tea exception flow throws a cancel event, which implicitly causes all compensators to trigger. The cancel event is also caught on the transaction subprocess border, leading to the final activity, "Throw away stale tea." When all of the compensators complete, the exceptional flow, resulting from the cancel event, should automatically be triggered.

Figure 4.21 makes extensive use of the event subprocess to notify stakeholders of the status of ongoing tasks. The process loops through a set of records and validates the record with a decision in DMN, additionally performs a task associated with the record. If an error occurs, such as if the data attributes were inadequate or there was a business rule violation, then the error can be corrected. At the second level of errors the entire set of records is reversed or rolled back.

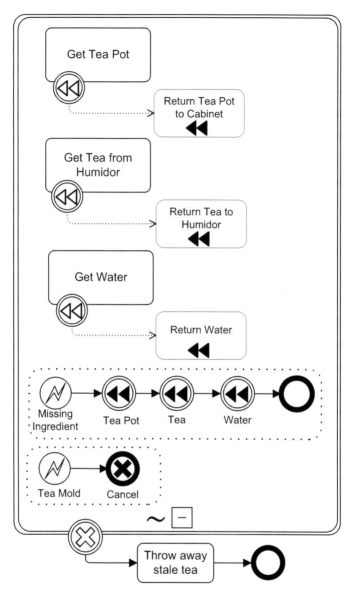

Figure 4.20 *Transaction subprocess containing compensation events and associated compensation handler activities.*

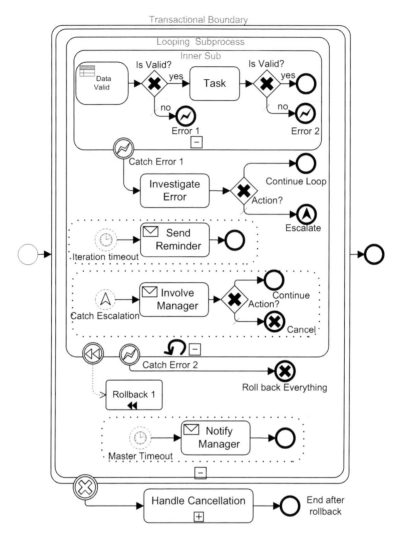

Figure 4.21 *A combination of event subprocess and boundary event handlers for decision-driven errors.*

DECISION LOGIC IMPLEMENTATION

Chapter 3 introduced the decision modeling use case of developing a complete decision requirements diagram and then extending that diagram with decision logic so that it can be executed. This section contains some suggestions for working with more advanced decision logic constructs in DMN.

FEEL

The most obvious way in which a more detailed specification for the implementation of decision logic can be developed is the use of FEEL—the Friendly Enough Expression Language. FEEL is defined in the DMN specification for those situations in which a precise definition of decision logic is required within a decision requirements model.

There are two variants of FEEL: Simple FEEL or S-FEEL and full FEEL. Using S-FEEL or FEEL allows the literal expressions of decisions or business knowledge models to be written more formally, rather than simply using natural language or structured English. In principle, a decision requirements model where all the decision logic is expressed in S-FEEL or FEEL, including the decision logic embedded in a decision table, can be interpreted and executed by a BRMS.

S-FEEL

S-FEEL handles only simple expressions. It is ideal for use in decision tables where the structure of the decision table frames the logic. The combination of a decision table and S-FEEL allows a literal expression to be conveyed completely enough to be executed. A decision requirements model containing only invocations and decision tables with S-FEEL as literal expressions is both executable and easy to read.

S-FEEL supports all the standard arithmetic operators, assignments, and unary tests such as = and >, as well as the ability to check values against intervals, handle NOT, and others.

FEEL

Full FEEL adds a number of capabilities to S-FEEL. In particular, it allows modelers to define:

- Qualified names
- Parameters
- If/then/else condition structures
- Loops
- Text handling expressions
- ORs/ANDs
- Functions

With these additional capabilities, it is possible to define a block of decision logic for a decision or business knowledge model where a decision table cannot handle the complexity or where a more traditional schema simply works better. It also allows "glue" logic to be defined so that functions can be called and parameters can be mapped in ways that are less regular than can be supported by requirements and invocations.

Advanced Business Knowledge Models

Chapter 2 introduced the idea of business knowledge models as a container for reusable decision logic. Decisions that require a single business knowledge model can be represented by an invocation that maps the information requirements of the decision to the parameters of the business knowledge model.

However, it is possible to build a network of business knowledge models. Here, a business knowledge model invokes other business knowledge models. These invocations are shown using knowledge requirements on the decision requirements diagram. In practice, however, any such network is likely to require the use of FEEL in any decision or business knowledge model that invokes more than one business knowledge model.

Such a network can be used to manage alternative versions of decision logic suitable for different situations such as different formats for address handling, as well as to allow the definition of fine-grained blocks of reusable decision logic.

Mappings for the relevant data should be provided for each use of the business knowledge model. If the business knowledge model is used by a decision, then the information requirements of that decision—from input data and dependent decisions—must be mapped to the specific parameters of the business knowledge model. Where business knowledge models call each other, some of the data in the calling business knowledge model must be mapped to the parameters of the called business knowledge model so that it can be passed correctly at execution time.

Advanced Decision Tables

The basics of decision tables were introduced and described in Chapter 3. There are some additional, advanced elements of decision tables that are also supported by DMN.

Most decision tables use a variable per column (or per row when rules are represented in columns). The logic in the cell then applies to this variable, comparing it to a value, for example. Decision tables can also use an expression in place of a variable. This allows a row or column representing a condition to be based on an expression. A comparison or a calculation could be specified, for instance. The cells can then be marked as True/False (does the input expression evaluate to true or not) or can be combined with the input expression in some way (comparing a calculated input expression to a value, for example). When a comparative expression is used as an input expression, an *X* displayed in a decision table cell evaluates to true if the input expression of the cell evaluates to true.

Decision tables can also list the possible values for inputs and outputs. These values then constrain the values in the table. Described using one or more expressions per input variable (in S-FEEL, for instance), any value tested for must match one of the expressions. For example, several valid ranges could be described for an input variable, and a valid value would be one that was in one of the ranges. If output values are specified, they also determine the priority if tables of type P or O are used (see below).

Decision tables can have multiple output variables. When multiple output variables are defined, then each decision table result may include a value from each such output variable. Next, these are assembled into a compound object that should match the result of the decision or business knowledge model that uses the decision table.

Chapter 3 focused on some key hit policies for decision tables. For single hit tables, the core types are the "Unique" type (only one row/column can possible evaluate to true) and the "Any" type (all rows/columns that can evaluate to true at the same time, resulting in the same action). These are the most common and are the most robust, as the ordering of the rows/columns in the decision table does not affect the outcome. This is especially important when non-technical users regularly update a decision table to reflect evolving practices or policies.

It is possible, however, to also define single-hit tables that return a result based on rule Priority (the result from the highest priority of the rules that evaluates to true is used) shown with a *P* in the hit policy and on the First rule that evaluates true shown with an *F*. As both of these can end in different results when the table is reorganized, they should be used rarely and with care.

Multiple hit tables can produce their results in:

- No order, where nothing can be assumed about the order the hits are returned in.
- Output Order, where the hits are returned in the order specified by list of allowed output values.
- Rule Order, where the hits are returned in the order the rules are written in the table.

Generally, with multiple hits, it is important to think of the results as a set, not a sequence. Therefore, No Order is preferable, and the others should be used rarely and with care. The exact way in which multiple hits are aggregated is also defined and can include building a collection, summing, determining min or max, counting, or averaging. Generally, only collecting all the results, sum, and count have strong use cases, and anything else should be handled by post-processing the output of the table to avoid ambiguity.

Decision tables may also be marked as Complete using a *C* to show that they produce a result in all circumstances. This is the default, however, so if there are circumstances in which no result can be determined, the table should be marked as Incomplete with an *I*.

Other Decision Logic Representations

While DMN only defines decision tables as formal representations for decision logic, it also recognizes that not every decision's logic might be represented in this way. When working with a tool that supports DMN, a modeler may be able to specify the decision logic of a decision or a business knowledge model using some other representation. Examples include predictive analytic models, decision trees, and other non-table rule formats.

Predictive analytic model

A decision or business knowledge model can be described using the Predictive Model Markup Language (PMML). PMML is an industry standard extensible markup language (XML) format for describing predictive analytic models. To specify that a PMML model should be used in this way, the body of the decision or business knowledge model is expressed in PMML, and a type *P* (for PMML) is specified for the function. The parameters specified for the business knowledge model or the information requirements of the decision should match those specified for the PMML model. When the decision or business knowledge model is invoked, the relevant data elements will be mapped to these parameters and passed to the PMML model for execution.

Decision trees

Decision trees are a common representation of decision logic and a very powerful one in the right circumstances. For example, segmentation of a population into groups can be very clearly represented as a decision tree. At present, there is no way to represent such a tree in DMN.

Instead, modelers could use a preferred graphic representation for the tree for editing. The rules implied by the tree can be represented as a set of rules written in FEEL for execution. Future releases of DMN are likely to support a standard decision tree format.

Other non-table formats

Many BRMS tools provide other editing metaphors for business rules. When it makes sense to use these, modelers can take a similar approach, managing them using their preferred graphical layout and using FEEL to represent the underlying execution semantics of the rules.

ADVANCED DECISION REQUIREMENTS DIAGRAMS

Besides the core use cases for decision requirements diagrams defined in Chapter 2, there are a couple of less common use cases that are worth noting.

Advanced Authority Requirements

Most authority requirements link a decision to the knowledge sources on which it is based or link a business knowledge model to the knowledge sources on which its logic is based. In both cases, the link shows the authorities for the decision logic being represented. Additional, less common use cases for authority requirements include:

- Knowledge sources can act as authorities for other knowledge sources. This can be used to show a hierarchy of policy documents or regulations, for example.

- Input data can act as an authority for a knowledge source to show analytic derivation. Where the knowledge source is analytic know-how, such as the results of data mining or a set of predictive analytic insights, it can be very helpful to show the input data that is analyzed to produce them. This allows the chain from decision to analytic knowledge source to input data to be followed outside of the execution semantics of the decision.

- A decision can act as an authority for a knowledge source. This is generally used where a decision is periodically made as to the content of a knowledge source. For instance, a monthly decision is made regarding a risk policy. The policy is a knowledge source, and the decision is part of what determines its value. Similarly, a decision to pick a champion or challenger strategy might impact a knowledge source.

As with all authority requirements, these have no impact on execution and should be used only when doing so adds clarity.

Analytic Requirements

It has been stated earlier that a literal expression could be an analytic model, represented perhaps using PMML. In this way, the decision making represented by a decision requirements model is not limited to decision logic that can be represented in tabular rules-based formats but can be extended to include algorithmic decision making. This is an important characteristic of decision requirements models developed in DMN.

Alternatively, decision requirements models can be used to specify requirements for analytic projects. The decision making the analytic project is intended to improve can be defined, and the analytic insight itself can be modeled as a knowledge source. The knowledge source can be linked back to the original input data it was derived from.

In this way, a decision model can be developed to provide business context for a data mining or predictive analytic model development process. For instance, the widely used CRISP-DM approach (Cross Industry Standard Process for Data Mining) identifies understanding business objectives and understanding —Business Understanding—as the first phase in a project. A decision model for the decision to be improved is ideal for this purpose.

Not only does this integrate the analytic requirements into the model, it also allows the modeler to show exactly how and where the analytic will be consumed in the decision making. Decisions are linked to objectives and performance indicators showing what the business value of improvements in this knowledge source would be.

Advanced Information Requirements

When decomposing decisions, there are a number of specific situations to consider. There is no standard notation for any of these.

Optional Sub-Decisions

Not all the sub-decisions required by a decision are required every time the decision is made. Optional decisions, required by some transactions, should also be modeled. Often, it is helpful to have one diagram with the "required" decisions and a more detailed one with optional decisions.

Circumstantial Variation

Related to optional decisions, sometimes a decision has different requirements in different circumstances. When there is this kind of circumstantial variation, the overall decision is going to require a sub-decision that determines which of the various circumstances is true.

Multiple Occurrences of Sub-Decision

Sometimes a decision requires a sub-decision to be made more than once. For instance, a decision about an invoice might require a decision about an invoice line, and that decision is taken multiple times for each invoice decision. There is no notation for showing this multiplicity, but it should be noted in the supporting text.

SUMMARY

For BPMN, the basics of complex gateways, error event, escalation event, transitions, compensations, and cancels were covered. With the information in this chapter, modelers should almost be able to develop nearly execution-ready processes. The final steps are described in Chapter 9, model to execution.

In BPMN, handling errors arising from a subprocess is known as "exceptional flow," and for errors, this is always interrupting: the subprocess that generated the error will terminate, and the alternate "exceptional flow" is followed. This can be handled with either an event subprocess or a subprocess boundary. In the latter case, the process can merge exceptional flow with the main flow. The exceptional flow merge does not need to immediately return to the subprocess that generated the error. If required, a process model can merge several steps downstream.

Decisions are critical for determining if errors exist, not only for the existence of the error but also for the corrective actions that need to be taken to fix the error. If subprocesses are created with the error-checking steps, business rules would be placed into BPMN, which is not the recommended approach.

The process of defining a standardized set of exceptions processes can be implemented as an event subprocess, and this can be reused across many processes. These can be important for creating standard responses to infrastructure errors/ITIL. These can be added throughout the execution system to standardize the response to unhandled exceptions in the process.

With this last chapter on BPMN/DMN shapes, this completes the review of shapes.

The key to understanding BPMN notations is in the conventions of the markings. For example:

- Activities and subprocesses are rounded rectangles. Transaction subprocesses are double lined. Event subprocesses have dotted lines.
- Events are drawn as circles. The inner shape (e.g., message, escalate, timer) is the same regardless of the outer circle type.
- Events that are thrown are shown with black markers; catching events are white.

Starting events are denoted with thin circles, and ending events are denoted with thick circles. Intermediates are always double-lined.

- Non-interrupting events are dashed circles instead of solid.
- Exit a subprocess via the boundary event. The chapter covered some considerations of how error events and non-interrupting events should be modeled.

This chapter's focus is on handling complexity. Process modelers must decide which style to use. It is recommended that modelers use a high-level diagram with few details first, as in Chapters 2 and 3. In particular, a focus on decisions, as in Chapter 2's DMN, is helpful. This chapter defines a more mature, production-ready process, yet there are steps that must be taken to build an executable process. This is covered in Chapter 7.

This chapter explored some of the advanced characteristics of DMN, including FEEL and S-FEEL, and expanded the understanding of the decision table and rules for the evaluation of decision tables. This chapter also discussed more advanced forms of business knowledge. As the decision models become more mature, modelers will need to add these concepts to their decision models. This chapter also discussed alternate forms of representing logic.

The remainder of the book will briefly explore process modeling in BPMN/DMN in the context of decisions, business logic, and events. As mentioned in the introduction, process modeling in BPMN/DMN is a very powerful problem solving tool. Yet, it is just one part of an integral view of the goals and objectives of the organization. There are other metaphors, namely, decisions and events that will completely detail the activities of the organization's process.

CHAPTER 5

BUSINESS EVENTS AND
BUSINESS EVENT MODELING

INTRODUCTION

The business event is one of the three principal process modeling metaphors. The event-centric process is a critical process usage pattern. Regardless of the process usage pattern, events, just like decisions, are universally relevant throughout every enterprise. The events focused on in this chapter are significant occurrences, mostly beyond the boundaries of the enterprise that affect its processes. These can be environmental, such as a weather shift, or economic, such as a change in commodity availabilities. More events might arise from political or social sources.

Event-based process modeling creates processes that are more aware. Hugh Brown et al. state that, "Events…bring consciousness to the enterprise nervous system."[1] Enterprise business events happen all the time. The challenge is to understand how some events are relevant to business processes and how these events affect the outcome of processes.

By definition, companies with the best conscious awareness of events are the most competitive. Like the butterfly effect from chaos theory, seemingly minor, secondary (micro) changes can have a quick and disruptive (macro) effect on business operations. Events signal changes that can profoundly affect products, services, customers, employees, and risk exposures. Only recently has the power of adapting to external change through event thinking become a critical aspect of process modeling.

Event thinking is a shift from a focus on the internal processes to a focus on the external non-process elements. Both viewpoints are reasonable and present

---

1. Hugh Brown, et al. *Event-Driven Architecture: How SOA Enables the Real-Time Enterprise.* Addison-Wesley Professional, 2009.

different viewpoints of the same objective, the progress of enterprise activities over time.

- The process viewpoint depicts a preconceived map of activities with a set of pre-planned sequences. The process model is composed of activities, sequences, gateways, and other elements.
- The non-process viewpoint focuses on distribution of states, random events, decisions, and activities.

In either view, the activities of the enterprise are identical. Yet a process is an organization of things that should happen in a proscribed sequence. As a process becomes more rigid and organized, fewer unexpected events can be accommodated. There are two new distinctions:

- It is possible for activities and responses to be expressed as a collection of organized events, often directed through decisions, but not necessarily as a process. This is called *complex event detection*.
- It is also possible to have a disorganized process with no event sequence. This is called an *ad hoc process*.

For business analysts, the event is a natural focus of a use case. Also, events accurately describe the phases of processes. Customer events include orders, receipts, payments, and returns. Similarly, supplier events include deliveries and invoices. With previous methodologies, these orders, receipts, and others would have been data elements, objects, and process activities. In BPMN, they can be events. A process should be a natural flow of events: customer's orders lead to shipments, which lead to customer receipts.

The difference in process and non-process viewpoints can be seen in the following basic process fragment:

In Figure 5.1, the transition from the first activity to the second activity is presupposed or hardwired.

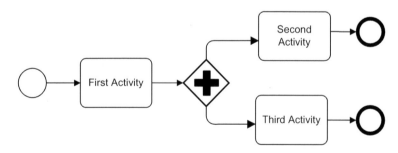

Figure 5.1 *A simple process fragment with a gateway.*

However, in Figure 5.2, intermediate message events were added that would emerge from a cloud of events and start the second or third activity. In the next activity, the actions of the organization would be the same, but the transition to the second activity would be initiated with decision, followed by a message flow that emerges from a consideration of external events. The decision is the mechanism of consideration. The difference with this approach is in the controlling logic that is monitoring events. Starting logic for the second activity could use internal and external events as input. Activities in the event-driven or non-process viewpoint are not predetermined; they are a part of a grid of potential event responses. Herein lies the dynamic nature of more dynamic processes.

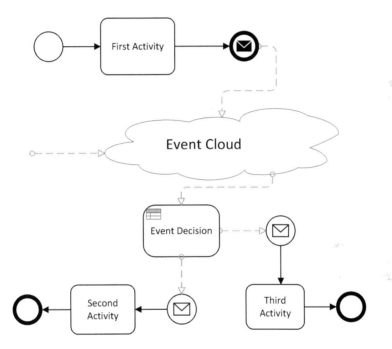

Figure 5.2 *Internal processes controlled by decisions from the external cloud of events.*

An event process environment is different than a business process environment. BPMN shapes might be used to design processes to anticipate conditions that might prevent the second or third activities from taking place; however, the process design or the DMN logic must be changed to accommodate design changes.

Since events are not neatly organized, David Luckham[1] created the cloud analogy for the event space. According to Luckham, "[Events] do not necessarily

arrive at the enterprise in the order they were created or in their causal order…
they form an unorganized cloud of events."

Beyond sending a message to a process, Figure 5.2 raises a number of important issues. For example, how will the event capability decide what events to send to the processes? Can a process contribute events to the cloud? This chapter will touch on event processing as it relates to the process.

Ultimately, many advanced processes will consolidate all events into a single layer for maximum visibility and positioning for change. This centralizes control of critical events, and because event monitoring is continuous and controlled by decision logic, rules-driven process control is also achieved.

This chapter introduces the effective and efficient methods needed to identify and address requirements arising from business events. First, to understand how business events are modeled, decision and decision logic must be understood. Then, events analysis constructs the requirements for business event processing. To support business responses and decision making processes, event-driven processes leverage the information flowing through business systems and IT.

BUSINESS EVENT PROCESSING

Business event processing is a relatively new enterprise component. Nearly all components share the ability to recognize an event, decide that an actionable business situation has occurred, and coordinate the appropriate response (action). Event processing applies decision logic in the form of rules to one or several events, with the purpose of identifying the material events within the event cloud. Event processing detects, filters, correlates, and directs the appropriate messages to the correct channel. For example, in an electric car owner's request for a charging point, an event processing decision point would seek an open slot (detect) and apply decision logic to the opening (assignment). In other scenarios, an event message could indicate that a commodity has reached critical price points, a trading partner is experiencing financial stress, or a security detector was activated.

Business Events Notation

Drawing on the previous chapters, a graphical depiction of basic event-processing concepts is shown in Figure 5.3.

Figure 5.3 shows an event detection entity and two calls to reusable decision models. The oval denotes continuous event monitoring and detection. Stateless logic filters and correlates the detected event. Events are then directed to the correct channel for receipt by a process.

---

1. David Luckham. *The Power of Events: An Introduction to Complex Event Processing in Distributed Enterprise Systems.* Addison-Wesley Professional, 2002.

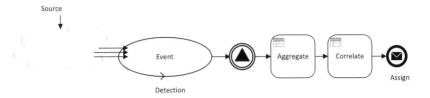

Figure 5.3 *Concepts of the atomic functions of event processing.*

In addition to business events, millions of potentially actionable events are flowing freely through the IT infrastructure. Since the proper response to these events is critical, event analysis is an essential part of process modeling.

Supporting the need for advanced event processing is a new and growing discipline. Organizations use the event-centric process pattern to interact and respond to a growing volume of business events and transactions in an agile, proactive way. Event analysis is an emerging area of business process modeling that develops support for the decision-based processing of events significant to the enterprise. Since events can be produced by devices, it is also an increasingly vital part of strategies for the evolving IoT. The need for external event processing has increased as processes are discovered, mapped, and managed.

Business processes must accommodate event-driven, actionable situations. These include key events or combinations of events. The process model should be constructed to respond with the correct sequence of activities.

A thorough discussion of EDA is beyond the scope of this book; however, the relationship between process modeling, BPMN, DMN, the EDA, and a number of business scenarios that implement event processing for improved decision making will be discussed.

Event Processing Overview

At a rental car agency, changes in rental car inventory are common. But these events do not necessarily affect everyone. Perhaps loyalty customers would receive an opportunity for a free upgrade when inventory levels are adequate. Various communications update customers regarding their reservations. To improve processes and customer loyalty, most car rental companies offer upgrade availability status notification to their gold customers. In this case, an email is sent or a phone call is made. Specific, relevant information is sent to the customer (a process participant) with direct access to menu items to take action.

As in the car rental example, a modern, complex business process should be modeled with consideration for how events that affect processes are distributed. Choosing the event-decision pattern is important to understanding the nature of the process and to achieving optimal efficiency. Sometimes an event needs to have guaranteed delivery to one or more participants. This requires a message. Other times, guaranteed delivery will require too much traffic. In such a case, a broadcast can be used to notify any potentially interested participants. Later in this chapter, a pattern to assist with appropriate event notification type choice will be introduced.

Chandy and Schulte[1] define the business event as "an event that is meaningful for conducting commercial, industrial, and governmental or trade activities." An event is Boolean in nature; it either happened (True), or it did not (False). More importantly, an event is not only data, but it is also relevant to a point in time. The event is meaningful because it might affect a business process as an external message or channel, which one or more processes must consume, activate, and respond to.

Chapters 3 and 4 described BPMN events. The events discussed here are external business events. Processes in BPMN can be built that mimic, looping for events and evaluating conditions, the functions of an event-processing environment. However, BPMN alone does not fully describe the needed technical capabilities. Nonetheless, it can and will be used to describe event-based processes, which are activated by or respond to the event-processing facility.

An occurrence of an event will be called an *event instance*. An event instance is uniquely identified by event processing throughout an application or system and acts as a canonical key.

Regarding event process modeling, there are three categories of events:

- Ordinary, trivial business process events, including activity transitions, message flows, and anticipated errors and exceptions.
- External Business Events (EBEs): In combination with business rules, these provide channels for messages in BPMN business processes. For example, a purchase order has been issued through an X12 EDIFACT file, yet critical equipment has been recalled by the manufacturer, and sensor data has reached a limit.
- Internal Business Events (IBEs): These can arise from the IT infrastructure, and BPMN is particularly adept at handling these.

The last two categories, EBE and IBE, require that processes respond and react to these business events. Not only are events detected and processed, but they can also affect in-flight processes.

IBEs and EBEs form the global cloud of events which feed decision models. They are referenced indirectly in the OMG Business Motivation Model. IBEs and EBEs emerge from the influencers' portion of the model. Internal influencers can

---

1. K. Mani Chandy and W. Roy Schulte. *Event Processing: Designing IT Systems for Agile Companies.* McGraw-Hill Osborne Media, 2009.

be assessed to be strengths or weaknesses, and an internal event such as reaching or missing a key performance indicator can be one of these. External influencers, which are counted as opportunities and threats, are analyzed as parts of the business plan. The external events mentioned above, such as critical equipment recalled or sensor data reaching a limit, might be influencers.

An assessment is defined by the term. It is a judgment about some type of influencer. An influencer becomes active when the enterprise decides how to respond to it. The business process or business rules that react to or process the event is connected to an assessment of the event and to the conjunction of the means and ends of the model.

An event producer or source produces events. Event producers can be as broad as financial market indexes or government economic indicators, or they can be as small as a temperature sensor. Event producers are often a combination of many individual producers. Additionally, business event producers can be external to the organization. Their origins are broad-ranging and random. For example, a targeted, external event producer might be a trading partner's application, service, or business process. In IoT, the producer can be a detector, a sensor, or a social networking or email application.

With an event processing method, raw EBEs are recognized at the source. Upon sensing an event, a decision or decision model must apply logic that leads to an appropriate outcome. This logic can also evaluate conditions against broader event processing patterns or higher orders of logic that correlate current or past events with desired outcomes. Such a decision might reference PMML to include predictive analytic models and provide analytic decision making.

Decision outcomes can either control a business process or publish an event. Capturing and tracking the event for historical purposes is also beneficial.

EVENT ANALYSIS

There are three components to event modeling, identification of:

1. Event producers, feeds from external systems, monitors of internal systems.
2. Event-processing decision logic in decision models.
3. Event consumers processes in the enterprise that must respond.

Analysts need to identify the relationships between producers, decision logic, and consumers. In many cases, an event handler is a grid or a networked collection of interacting events, and the analyst will work across the grid to build up the relationships. In this context, the primary objective of event analysis would be to decide event producers, event characteristics, and the decision logic needed to process the events and deliver the output to the consumers.

A detected event generally moves through a number of phases prior to being placed on an event channel. Part of event analysis is to determine the phases and the controlling logic.

Types of Event Processing

Event processing falls into various levels of complexity. CEP uses a pattern to identify events. A patterned analysis might span many, possibly millions, of independent conditions and events. Examples of these events might include market abuse, cyber warfare, or changes in trading patterns for market equities. A CEP pattern is a collection of conditions or constraints that indicate the occurrence of an event. CEP patterns might involve many causal, temporal, and spatial dimensions. Despite the complex and rich nature of the information used by CEP, the output is simple: business events that require a response.

As already mentioned, not all event processes need CEP. Some processes are singular, or a node on a grid of events. Examples of simple events can be simple business transactions, medical records, or supply chain transactions processing. Usually the transactions within a process are related, such as a shipping receipt for a purchase order or a bid for a request for proposal. Ordinary, grid events are filtered, correlated, and routed with little modification other than attribute ornamentation. Correlation might look for related prior events or anticipated future events. As each event happens, decision logic is applied, and each event occurrence is routed to the event consumer through a channel. The transformation might then route events. It might merge them with other events, as in a shipment receipt. Then, simple decision logic might translate the events schema into a canonical form. This type of event processing provides the utilities needed by CEP.

Event processing can incorporate analytics and intelligent decision management techniques to predict events and mime patterns.

Event Processing and Business Process Models

Business event processing and business process modeling with BPMN/DMN can create an effective combination of timely event pattern detection and dynamic business process execution. Business event processing simplifies the construction of the event-driven business process usage pattern. Event processing with DMN identifies and channels business situations (as actionable) and signals the business process to respond. Additionally, even though there are no standards for event processing, many products support graphical, non-procedural user interfaces that business analysts and managers use to define the event processing interactions and actions.

EVENT MODELING FRAMEWORK (EMF)

As mentioned in the book introduction, modern processes are constructed with the three metaphors: business processes, decisions, and events. Each of these metaphors has a perspective, logical components, and a design framework.

The Event Modeling Framework (EMF) develops and connects the three key event processing concepts:

1. Event-sensing or detecting functions for input events.
2. Event decision logic.
3. Event channels for consuming processes.

The framework is independent of the technologies that process events. Yet all technologies share attributes similar to the ones described here.

The goal of the EMF is to create the fabric of event processing systems and event-driven business processes and to provide a common framework for specifying event processing solutions and implementations.

Event Decision Logic

In the EMF, there are several classes of decisions for event processing which usually occur in the following order:

1. Detection
2. Distribution
3. Aggregation
4. Correlation
5. Assignment

Not every event processor includes all of these steps. Also, except for detection, which comes first, it is not required for these steps to be executed in this order. The list shown is theoretically ideal for all event processing situations.

> **Detection:** In event detection, decision logic is applied to data monitored by the event detector. A business-relevant event or event of interest is discovered when the event process matches the logic with the data. For example, perhaps the detected events are equity prices that fall within a specific percentage. For ordinary events, logic detects the equity that is of interest and whether the percentage falls within the prescribed limit.
>
> **Distribution:** In event distribution, the detected event is immediately alerted to the affected process or systems according to the logic and levels of participation. Most organizations have four levels of participant

involvement: active, passive or monitoring, informational, and uninformed. Decision logic decides the level of involvement and the destination of the distributed event. Distribution logic can be simplistic, such as a burglar alarm during irregular hours. Complex distribution logic might deliver the event based on the scale of the data within the event. For example, a delivery order of a special size for a contract might need a distinct process.

Events are distributed through two distinct patterns, either through a message or a broadcast. The message corresponds to the BPMN message. Event processing targets the event-activated messages at a process instance. The broadcast distribution method is denoted as a signal event in BPMN and is analogous to a radio signal. While a message persists until acknowledged, a broadcast is only relevant for a short period of time. An undelivered message might require reattempts to deliver, but unnoticed signal events are simply discarded. Furthermore, messages contain a payload of data, whereas a signal is more likely an event that prompts a participant to retrieve data.

If the broadcast and message patterns are used properly, it will be easy to optimize process and event models.

Aggregation: Many business events are only meaningful when they are combined with other events of a similar or related nature. Logical significance might arise from the timing or temporal nature of the other events. In aggregation, event processing uses business rules logic to identify significant events from a group of events. For example, an instance of suspected market abuse might be created by an aggregation of similar trades or trades that are suspiciously timed. Business rules define the logic of the similarity and the timing.

Correlation: Event processing always includes a correlation step. The introduction explained how event processing can play a role in the application-centric usage pattern by detecting internal or external events and correlating these with concurrent processes or data in the enterprise. Active business processes might be identified as intended recipients. For instance, if a vendor fails to certify lab testing during an ongoing testing program administration, a decertification event can raise an exception in a running process. Decision logic defines what data or process states are included in the correlations and logic of the match.

Assignment: At the conclusion of the cycle in assignment, the event is assigned to one or more processes. Decision logic can choose which process is assigned to the event for action. As with all rules, the assignment can be as straightforward as the unconditional assignment to a single process, or it can be a time, capability, and dependent assignment.

As shown in Figure 5.4, event processing proceeds in a cyclical fashion until one of the processing steps consumes or replaces another.

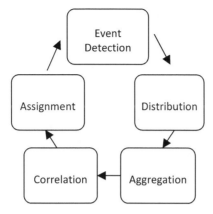

Figure 5.4 *Event processing proceeds until the event is consumed or replaced by another processing step.*

BPMN/DMN can also describe this type of event processing—for instance, if an event process needs to detect, aggregate, correlate, and assign. The process shown in Figure 5.5 depicts the corresponding BPMN notation.

In this diagram, broadcast events are actively monitored. When a matching signal meets the event criteria (broadcast signal attributes match), the process is triggered. A script is run to match new signal data with what exists in a data source. The decision logic referenced by the rule call determines the action to take, such as data assignment, or if any participants should directly receive the event. The current state (e.g., moving average, status, standard deviation) is updated as a service task.

Event Channel

An event channel publishes, signals, or posts events and streams of events as process instances. Traditionally, event processing is complete once the event has been directed to a channel. In more advanced approaches, as shown in Figure 5.4, the event might continue to be processed.

In the assignment or distribution steps, the event channel might transmit multiple events from different event processes. Alternately, it might combine events from many processes. Event decision logic should handle ordering among the events from different processes to create the combined set of events. Again, the looping nature of event processing creates the order of events.

Within BPMN, two active shapes respond to event channels: the message and the signal. There are three event cycle phase shapes, which are summarized in

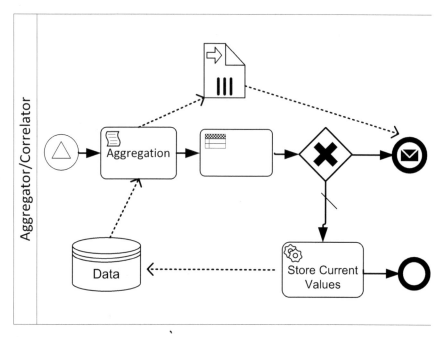

Figure 5.5 *Event interceptor, aggregator, correlator, and assigner.*

Table 5.1. In an event processing step, the logic conditions detect, aggregate, and correlate are depicted as one condition.

Figure 5.6 shows a BPMN model of a detector and distributer. A condition is detected, resulting from multiple events and data states. When detected, a signal is broadcast to any interested participants.

Event Repository

Most event scenarios connect with a previous process instance or related event. For instance, a power outage event in a smart grid might not be meaningful if it has a very short duration. A single outage of less than a second might be considered as a temporary glitch. However, a large number of short power outages, in combination with other events, could have a different meaning than a long or perpetual event. This might indicate an eminent equipment failure or the need to add capacity to the system. For this reason, an important responsibility of an event processing environment is to record the history of the events flowing through for retrospective analysis and processing.

Decision logic associated with event retention policies determines the duration and filtering conditions for retained events. The presence and timing of the information in the repository feed the business rules of the detection, aggregation, and correlation states. This logic is integral to the objectives of event processing.

Table 5.1 BPMN Shapes that Respond to Messaging in Event Processing

Event Cycle Phase	Symbol	Participant Involvement	Usage
Distribution	◯△	Informational/ Monitoring/ Screening	Broadcast a message continuously. Participants are responsible for actively monitoring broadcast channel. No guarantee of delivery of signal to participant. No persistence of signal.
Detection, Aggregation, Correlation	◯☰	Not involved/ Passive	Matches business events and data conditions to a process. Aggregates and filters events so that only relevant triggers start/resume the process.
Assignment	◯✉	Activates a participant	Triggers a participant to start/ resume a process. Contains the detailed data or instructions. Relies on external detection and correlation. Intended for a specific, single participant.

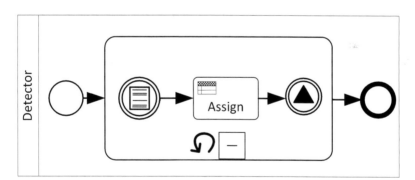

Figure 5.6 *Event detector, assignment logic, and distributor.*

Figure 5.7 depicts some concepts of the events that are placed in the repository. Event logic might need to identify a significant event. The repository records are stored automatically under the hood.

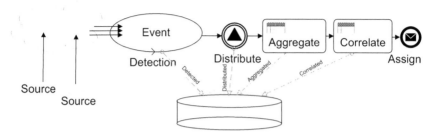

Figure 5.7 *The event repository concept is a critical part of event processing.*

BPMN SHAPES RELEVANT TO EVENT-CENTERED PROCESSES

Business events can start, stop, or interrupt processes. As such, many BPMN shapes can respond to an event-processing channel. Table 5.2 presents these shapes and their use with business events.

BUSINESS EVENTS USAGE PATTERNS

The chapter introduction suggested that there are five basic patterns for business events. In general, these patterns fall within the sequence of event processing and activities shown in Figure 5.8.

Figure 5.8 depicts a process distributing an event that is assigned through decision logic. The event receiver is the connection of the event to the business process. The concepts from the middle of the diagram find events and decide which participants to assign to take action. The qualified business event meets a business process that takes action on those events. As is typical practice, the assigned or distributed processes are designed to also look for things to do when no events are received. The timer acts as a backup check to verify that everything is working. For example, on a weekly basis, it may create a report. If anything interesting is found on the report, it may start the process.

The examples of event-driven process patterns follow:

> **Opportunistic:** A pattern of combined events that create another event that starts or alters the course of a business process.
>
> **Scenario:** A retail company wants to draw a customer into a store with customized offerings. The shopper that is near a store is sent a customized coupon via SMS that is specific to the shopper's needs.

Table 5.2 BPMN Shapes Highly Relevant to Event Processing

Shape Category	Shape	Relation to Event Processing
Message Event		As in each of the types in this table, the start, stop, intermediate, and non-interrupting messages are relevant to the business event. Event-based messages are used primarily for point-to-point integration of systems and are usually received by the assignment step in the process.
Signal Event		Used primarily for integrating systems that passively monitor each other's events. These processes use the signal as a condition or side effect. Signals arrive after event detection and distribution.
Condition Event		Used primarily as a monitor of process data. A logical rule or condition will trigger the condition event.
Multi Event		These shapes imply the usage of a channel (distribution or assignment) from an event processor. In the exclusive (pentagon) event, any one of multiple events can trigger the condition. For example, a commodity quote or an economic event will trigger this shape. In an inclusive event, all events must arise.

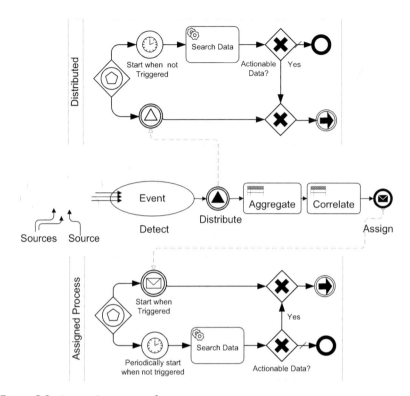

Figure 5.8 *A generic pattern of process response to events.*

The high-level event processing steps for this scenario include:

- Sources: Opt-in coupon subscribers, wireless carriers, geo-locators.
- Detect: Decide when subscriber is within a certain distance during store hours.
- Distribute: Alert customer tracking process that customer is within range.
- Aggregate: Customer's shopping behavior with current event.
- Correlate: Decide customer's preferences, identify if there are discounts available that match the customer's interests.
- Assignment: Decide which process generates and transmits the coupon.

The triggered processes include the customer location tracking and coupon generation.

Avoidance: A pattern of events designed for risk management objectives.

One scenario avoids financial and productivity losses that can be caused by the machines owned by a company. When important equipment is recalled or catastrophic defects are noted by news media, equipment managers are notified, and mitigating steps are taken.

The high-level event processing steps of avoidance include:

- Sources: Manufacturers, vendors of information, news feeds, legal announcements.
- Detect: Decide when equipment owned by the company is subject to bulletins, recalls, and/or lawsuits.
- Distribute: Alert equipment manager notification process, notify operators in the case of urgent recall.
- Aggregate: Decide the severity of recall and related recalls for the equipment.
- Correlate: Location and status of equipment.
- Assignment: Machine health maintenance management according to urgency.

The triggered processes include equipment manager notifications, operator notification, and maintenance management.

> **Notifying:** A pattern of events that trigger a flag or signal that will be observed by a person or a computer system.

One scenario notifies law enforcement when a license plate with a warrant or law enforcement code is detected. Law enforcement agencies use license plate detectors for increased efficiency, effectiveness, and public safety.

The high-level event processing steps include:

- Sources: License plate detectors.
- Detect: Decide when license plate is subject to investigation.
- Distribute: Alert central and local enforcement facilities.
- Aggregate: Determine the location of other alerts.
- Correlate: Locations and create projection of suspect movement and locations.
- Assignment: Case management for probation departments and law enforcement.

The triggered processes include direct notification of enforcement and case management.

Similar scenarios can be detailed and developed for the deviation and quantitative events types. For instance, market abuse is detected by deviation event types, and program trading in derivatives and hedges use the quantitative program types.

CONCLUSION

With event-based process modeling, processes become aware. Events bring consciousness to the enterprise nervous system. Business events decouple the process from the outside world yet allow the process to have "eyes and ears" to comprehend the business environment and respond to changes. The overall result is a more agile business model.

In summary, event processing connects events with decision logic and channels. Decision logic filters, processes, categorizes, and routes set off one or more events. In the final step, events are delivered to the right process consumers.

In general, event processing proceeds through five stages:

1.   Detection
2.   Distribution
3.   Aggregation
4.   Correlation
5.   Assignment

Event modeling offers a different view of the enterprise's relationship with its operating environment—the non-process viewpoint. This viewpoint sees the enterprises as a distribution of potential responses to events, states, and outcomes, as opposed to a process model's preconceived map of the sequence of activities.

The chapters on BPMN/DMN built an understanding of process and decision modeling by introducing a repertoire of shapes. A number of these shapes, specifically the message, signal, and multi-events, are well-suited to receive the channel output of event processing. When the use of these shapes in different scenarios is considered, it is evident that event processing can be used to create highly cooperative processes.

The requirements chapter will provide more details about verbally parsing business events. The approach advocated in the coming chapters is designed to work directly with a set of basic graphical notations. These empower managers and subject experts, and then process modelers and business decision modelers use these to build the solution.

CHAPTER 6

CONNECTING DECISIONS IN DMN TO PROCESSES IN BPMN

INTRODUCTION

The introduction suggested that the combination of decision modeling in DMN and process modeling in BPMN would create lighter, more focused processes by moving decision details into DMN. Using DMN alongside BPMN increases clarity and reduces the number of process gateways and script assignments, as well as the need for complex access to data sources.

A decision-driven process acts on the outcome of the evaluation of decision logic in several possible ways, including:

- Changing the sequence of activities that are taken after a decision, including what the next activity or process that is required to meet the directive of the process.
- Selecting between the paths on the diverging or the splitting side of a gateway.
- Deciding who or what participant should perform the needed activity.
- Creating data values that will be consumed later in the process.

As mentioned in previous chapters on handling complexity and event modeling, inputs into the decision include:

- Data that can identify events or process-relevant conditions.
- Data that must be validated for correctness.
- Data used in calculations.

In a way, the decision can be thought of as a meta gateway with merging inputs (events and data) and splitting outputs that direct the process in an overarching way (i.e., participants, tasks, and gateways) .

This new approach to process modeling includes decision modeling. Combining business process modeling with decision modeling, as well as event processing, can create comprehensive, agile solutions in many problem domains. Without decision modeling, process modeling in BPMN can both overcomplicate a model with logic and miss critical design details. As decisions are modeled, things will be discovered that the process must do to accommodate the results of those decisions. Exploring decisions will lead to the discovery of implicit process events, activities, and sequences.

This chapter will dissect a decision-driven use case based on transportation logistics and explore how the decision's outcome affects the process model. It will also explore how to parse the logic of the business case into expressions and decision tables.

The process models in this chapter are intended to support digitizing the business process. Other process modeling perspectives include organizational maturity and knowledge management, and BPMN can be used for this as well.

Decision modeling is a maturation of a legacy of practices by authors and thought leaders in the field of business rules. An accepted definition of business rules is:

"**Business rules** can be considered statements of the actions you should take when certain business conditions are true."[1]

When decisions are designed to direct digitized processes, dynamic rules are intended to be executed in a business rules management system and are written as expressions and decision tables connected to the model. As will be described later, not all business rules are part of modeled decisions. Many simplistic or static rules become elements of business processes. For instance, a rule that states, "payment processing must occur after product delivery," is expressed as two activities and a sequence.

A decision's outcome controls and directs pathways and other aspects of the process. The decision determines how the business will behave, and the behavior should be consistent with business rules related to compliance, operational, risk, and other objectives. A single decision can trigger and control multiple aspects of business processes, including events, activities, and data.

As shown in the diagram below, a common or naïve pattern for the outcome of responding to a decision is a control of a gateway diamond, or data-based gateway. Although efficient, streamlined decision behavior can control more process details.

---

1. Taylor, James, and Raden, Neil. *Smart (Enough) Systems: How to deliver competitive advantage by automating hidden decisions.* New York, NY: Prentice Hall, 2007.

Figure 6.1 depicts a gateway and the DMN model that provides output data to control the path or sequence of activities. The "Purchase Type" output from the decision is evaluated at the gateway and directs the path to the proper activity.

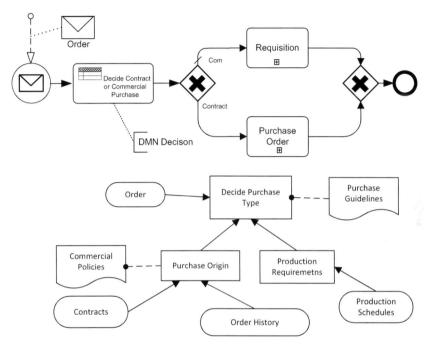

Figure 6.1 *Simple decision and gateway control of an execution path to respond to a purchasing decision.*

Process Discovery for Execution in DMN/BPMN

There are seven steps in a high-level process discovery effort using BPMN/DMN:

1. Develop a high-level process model. This high-level model and other discussions will help identify the critical decisions.
2. Identify decisions that support operational, compliance, and risk management objectives and that support these processes.
3. Develop decision models that show how to deliver the needed responses within these processes. In turn, these responses suggest process elements in an iterative development cycle.
4. A data model is necessary for executable decisions and processes. Develop a data model to provide specificity to process data elements and decision inputs/outputs.

5. The narrative of each decision allows for the refinement of the decision models, showing how multiple logic elements or conditions are combined.

6. Detailed decision logic can be specified to manipulate incoming data from input data sources or other decisions and produce the required outputs.

7. Use the assignment of values to attributes by decisions to prescribe downstream process components, activity order, role responsibility, paths through the process, data, and events.

The diagram below depicts five abstract, iconic processes patterns that highlight or illustrate the connection between the decision and the responding process. They suggest what can be affected with dynamic operational decisions.

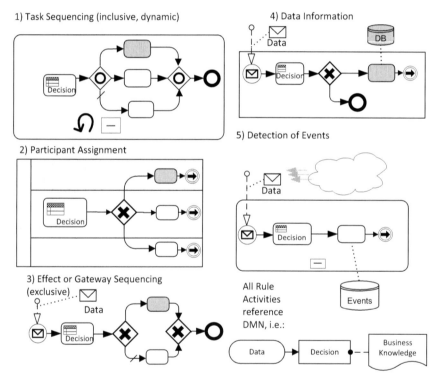

Figure 6.2 *Five categories of BPMN responses to decisions.*

Most process decisions' responses are a composite of these patterns. For example, a composite operational decision might affect both effect sequencing and actor inclusion. In addition to decision response requirements, the process is modeled as a composite of additional requirement inputs, such as orchestration with other systems and participants and technical infrastructure requirements.

Once high-level process and decision models are developed, the output artifacts can be prepared for an execution environment. This chiefly requires the addition of complete exception paths and connecting services and participants according to the technical architecture. We will cover the last step in Chapter 7.

Task Sequencing

In this scenario, the output data from a decision specifies, either explicitly or implicitly, the tasks that are executed by the business process. Often there are policies that dictate what a compliant process looks like. These policies add, re-order, or remove process elements. For instance, payment processing always follows shipment receipt. Decisions can dynamically control the sequence of activities, independent of static transitions.

There are many practical applications for this. Complex logic can trigger a sequencing of activities that are situationally aware. Complex products, customized services for customers, or manufacturing activities might need these abilities.

Figure 6.3 below shows a process fragment with an operational decision that explicitly decides the next phase of a dynamic inspection sub-process ("Quality Review," "Lab Testing," "Site Visit," or "Product Rejection"). The decision reviews the data and selects which step to take.

As with each of the examples of a process' response to operational decisions, the point of the pattern in Figure 6.3 is to demonstrate the concept, not necessarily to represent a full implementation.

In Figure 6.3, data from the output of the decision is evaluated in the condition of the gateway to select the next subprocess to execute. In the scenario, material that is inspected in an inspection process undergoes lab tests and other evaluation. Policies regarding the quality of the delivered material might require additional lab testing or a site visit. The data output from the selected activity is fed into the decision until the loops condition limit is reached, which is either an acceptance or rejection of the product.

The task sequencing pattern might take two forms:

- *Inclusive, parallel task sequencing*, where the evaluation gateway is data-based inclusive, and the decision might direct more than one task to occur.
- *Exclusive, sequential task sequencing*, where the evaluation gateway is data-based exclusive, and the decision might direct one or more tasks to occur.

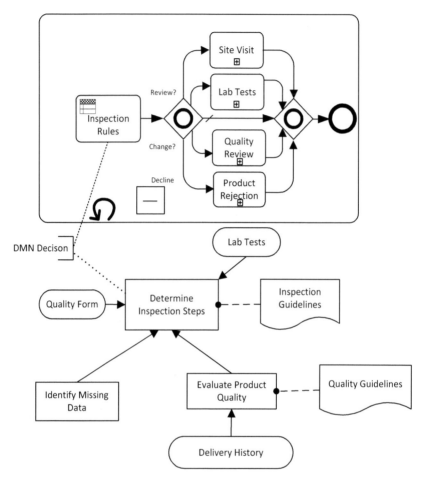

Figure 6.3 *The operational decision within the loop evaluates the result of an inspection and selects the next tasks, which might be run in parallel.*

There are other forms of dynamic process task assignments. With loops and nested inner loops, it is possible to specify a series or parallel set of tasks and decisions.

There are industry examples of this approach, including case management for legal due diligence and intellectual property applications. Applications that need adaptive case management (ACM) must sequence their activities according to the needs of the process instance. Here, activity steps might be redone or skipped. The logic for the ACM procedures can be placed in the operational decision. Another common use of this operational decision is within a nested checklist of completion items (punch list).

Participant Assignment

Decisions can dictate who or what roles are required to perform an activity. When an organization designs a process, participants might be static. Defined actors in the form of participants can be removed, added, or appointed to elements inside process lanes. Processes can also call a decision to dynamically delegate the activity to the correct actor to control what actor or participant performs an activity. Figure 6.4 depicts an operational decision that directs the outcome of an equipment calibration and repair request to a lane (role) in the process.

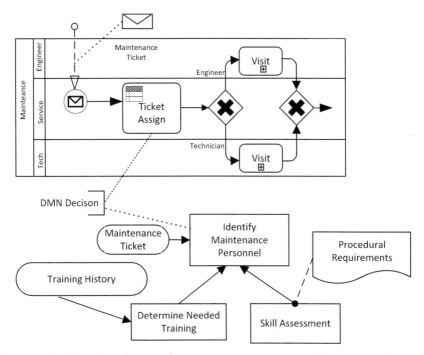

Figure 6.4 *Illustrating the second process response pattern 2, this process includes a decision that assigns a process participant to a part of the process.*

The decision in Figure 6.4 examines the contents of the maintenance ticket and determines the skills needed to complete the task. Two roles are available, Engineer and Technician. In addition, the decision ensures the available staff has current certifications to perform the needed maintenance. The maintenance ticket is the common input to the process and the decision. Output data is used at the gateways and in the activities to direct the process.

There are several forms of the participant assignment compliant process:

- Authority roles participant-based decisions where output of the decision dictates the role within a pool or a participant.
- Participant qualifications for training, certifications and other qualifications.

Beyond the limited security of the lane's role, operational decisions can discern the details of an activity and locate the correct person or group to conduct a task. In industrial or engineering services, personnel often must be certified to perform a task, and that certification can be time-limited. Other common uses for this type of operational decision include purchasing authority at different monetary values and types of legal reviews or oversights.

Effect Sequencing

Effect sequencing is the classic response to the outcome of a decision with the gateways of a business process. Figure 6.1 above illustrates this.

Most business processes contain multiple decision integration points. Processes can decide things like what risks are assigned to activities, what medical treatments apply to a patient, or which mode of communication is used. For these operational decisions, effect sequencing evaluates the process instance data.

Data Information

As shown in Figure 6.5, decisions can dynamically influence data validation. Dynamic decisions are excellent for validating data and for verifying the age and condition of the data. Decisions also decide things like storage durations and viewing authorizations to create a compliant process where internal controls govern how long recorded data is kept, the condition and state of complete or registered data, and who gets to see the data.

The process decision in Figure 6.5 evaluates the budget request in the form of an encumbrance. Two sub-decisions are made: the validity of the data and the availability of a budget allocation. The process loops until a valid record is entered.

Detection of Events

As shown in Figure 6.6, the final, and arguably most important, process-related function of a decision is event detection and control. Detection decisions select what processes or subprocesses should respond to business events. As defined earlier, business events can be external or internal. External business events might include customer or trading partner events. External events might also include more indefinite topics like weather, commodity, or security events. Internal busi-

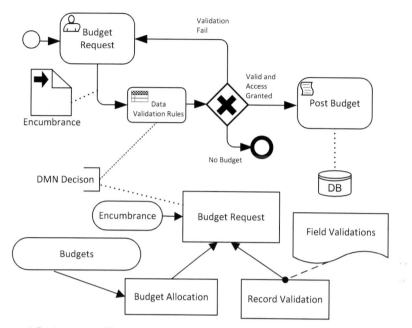

Figure 6.5 *A use case illustrating a decision validating data that is entered on a form.*

ness events arise from process activities such as when limiting conditions arise as in the need to order supplies, allocate more funds, or investigate errors.

Most often, with ordinary events, a process is statically designed and multiple layers of processing can be used: activities can be added, reordered, or removed. Processes can also respond to a business event dynamically. In Figure 6.6, a decision determines if the condition is reached and products need to be reordered.

Figure 6.6 considers the case when ordering materials for a type of equipment service. The repair kit sourcing decision examines the repair and a bill of materials for repair. To accelerate service times, a supply of the materials is kept in inventory, and when the inventory is low, a need for reordering is noted as an event to which a process must respond. This is shown in the non-interrupting escalation. If inventory falls to a threshold, a reorder process is started.

A detection decision uses the events to determine the action to take, such as assigning processes and participants. Detection decisions are used in several different situations, including:

- A step in an event processing channel where an incoming stream of messages must be properly responded to and processed.
- A step in processing a specific external event, such as monitoring weather risk services or commodity prices from a data service.

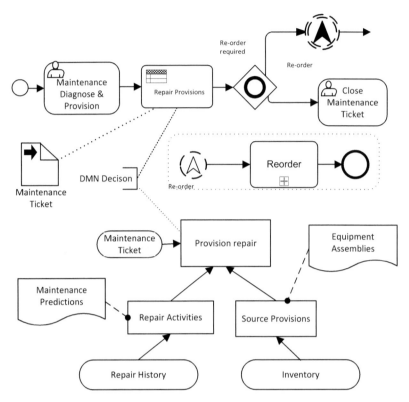

Figure 6.6 *This use case shows how a decision discovers that it is time to reorder supplies.*

As shown in the example below, decisions uncover important business events that must be handled. Consider these:

- Service employees need equipment to perform their tasks. When deciding what equipment to issue to an employee, an operational decision might consider the quantity needed and create a reorder business event.
- When servicing equipment, an operational decision assembles needed actions and discovers that a critical component is being replaced too frequently, triggering an investigation business event.
- When locating personnel to perform a task, an operational decision discovers that a person's training for an important capability has lapsed and triggers a training scheduling business event.

Frequently, in deciding a proposition concerning a process, limits are reached, funds are exhausted, and opportunities are identified.

EXPLORING A DECISION USE CASE

A supply chain logistics example can show how processes and decisions interact. A supply chain is a system of organizations, people, activities, information, and resources involved in moving a product or service from supplier to customer. Logistics is the management of the flow of goods between the point of origin and the point of consumption to meet requirements. This example looks at the activity of transporting material to a facility. This decision use-case covers nearly about every process-decision response, including gateways, roles, business events, and dynamic activities.

A chemical manufacturing company needs to manage a large number of shipments of various types of liquids, solids, and gases. These materials fall into various categories, including hazardous and non-hazardous. Some of the material which is considered particularly hazardous requires special handling and reporting. The material is sourced either from internal inventory, from contract sources, or from commercial purchases. To complete a shipment, the company starts with a material request that includes:

- The needed material and grade and quantities, including possible substitutions and combinations thereof.
- The shipment location(s) and delivery instructions, as well as available shipment modes.
- The shipment time frame(s).

The source of the material is the key decision. The objective of the decision is to obtain the material at the lowest laid down cost. This is the cost of the material from internal, contract, or commercial buys in addition to the transportation cost and handling and insurance fees.

Sources

There are three choices for sourcing the material:

1. *Internal sources:* Excess materials from cancelled batch runs is available, the unit price for this is established by the net of internal book value and disposal fees, and disposal fees are assessed against materials with a limited shelf life that are not likely to be consumed in a process.
2. *Contract sources:* The manufacturer contracts for the delivery of frequently used materials. Contracts serve a manufacturing area.

3.   *Commercial purchases:* Quotations can be obtained from certified vendors.

In most cases, there will be only one choice for materials sourcing.

Plant managers hold unused materials in inventory and assess a disposal fee and a disposal date. Because of high disposal costs, reuse of the material is promoted, and the price of the product can be negative.

No order can be placed against a lift on a contract that is set to end within 30 days of the scheduled delivery date. Delivery quantities cannot exceed the negotiated totals. If the current order brings the contract line item total within 90 percent of the line total, then the contract manager is notified to investigate a contract extension. Approval from the contract manager is needed if the contractor has two or more quality returns or bad lab tests within 90 days.

Frequently, commercial purchases are the only source for a material, so the company uses internal ordering decision processes to select which products to solicit contracts. If more than $200,000 of a material in a region is purchased within a 12-month time frame, then purchasing is directed to initiate contract solicitations. This solicitation is independent of the material sourcing.

Transportation

The selection of transportation is a combination of the lowest cost and the availability of insurance. The costs for transportation must be decided based on the size of the material order and delivery sizes of the transport medium. Where possible, quotations for contract purchases include transportation.

Gas transportation is more complex than this and requires special containers and other planning steps. Therefore, it will not be included in this scenario.

In some cases, the small fleet of company transportation can provide shipping at an economical cost. Online quotations are obtained for commercial carriers of all other forms.

Insurance

Input into the transportation decision is the liability insurance fee. A policy is selected from either existing coverage or special classes of hazardous materials that require special coverage riders.

Reporting

Various materials require different reporting processes in different states. The reports are driven by the product, the product category, and the state and transportation mode. The outcome of the decision tables is a list of processes that must be executed before the material shipment is decided and the transportation plan released.

For the purposes of this exercise, the insurance and reporting decisions will remain scaffolded.

DECISION SOLUTIONS IN DMN

The example has described the decisions that are needed to source and deliver the material. Each decision will be examined to determine the question that must be answered to make the decision. The question must be clear about the subject of the decision, timing, and the scope of the decision. The output of the question, the allowed answers, determines the process responses.

Remaining defining attributes include the organizational context, which are the KPIs and process or application that is impacted by the decision.

To develop the expressions and decision tables that implement these decisions, business rules are analyzed. Typical rules might include:

- Qualified vendor rules
- Defining active delivery orders
- Point of origin contract rules

Others terms of a constraint might build on these terms:

- Within the contract's certification period
- Acceptable payment performance
- Acceptable levels of defects

The actions that might be specified include:

- Deny Requisition
- Increase Liability Coverage
- Notify State Department of Environmental Protection

In other actions, the conditional terms can constrain who receives a material requisition or a discount on their order. To create a DMN expression, these concepts must be reduced to data and its derivation and interpretation. Data comes from the input to the decision, and in BPMN, its origin can be a process instance or enterprise data such as databases and operational data stores.

The outcome of the decision is an effect or influence of the process. Within a decision, some basic or unit operations might occur:

> **Categorize:** The type, sort, color, flavor, or division of the object is decided. This is generally done with a direct inspection of input data attributes.

Calculate: Formulas of data are applied, and statistics are developed. Values are determined, and these values can be assigned to a decision attribute.

Comparisons: Data is compared to redline, threshold value, or boundary conditions that are reached. Comparisons might also be made between the categorization and sets of categories.

Direct: The outcome of the expression, which might set the value of an expression, can direct the response of a process.

Categories of objects have already been mentioned in the list starting with qualified vendors. Other categories might include late shipments, damaged materials, and failed lab tests. Computations involving a metric, such as a lab test fail count, delivery quantity variance or date that characterizes a constraint.

Top Level Decision for Material Sourcing

At the highest level, a decision accumulates the results of the sub-decisions, answers the questions posed by the decision, and passes the resulting directives back to the calling process. A well-designed decision will apply all the logic that is needed to efficiently work with a business process: after the calling rule activity, other logic gateways are not used to call more decision activities.

The question for the material sourcing is:

> *How do we source and ship the material in the requisition in the manner that meets the production needs at the lowest laid-down price?*

Here are the allowed answers:

- Contract FOB origin purchase order and contract carrier
- Contract FOB destination using contracts shipment
- Commercial purchase and commercial transportation
- Commercial purchase and contract transportation
- Internal sources and commercial transportation
- Unable to source: Delay purchase and negotiate contract extensions
- Unable to source: Delay purchase and contract for purchase of material
- Unable to source: No contracts or certified vendors available

Note that FOB means free on board and refers to the point of purchase. Origin is at the designated facility, and destination is at the desired ship-to location.

The data from the decision hold attributes that detail the contract or vendor information and the relevant transportation information.

Data output by the decision will create a number of possible outcomes. As shown in Figure 6.7, the answer to the top-level decision does not always result in a source for the material and transportation. The data in the decision must decide the next activity, e.g., commercial requisition or contract purchase order. Additionally, the specific vendors and contracts are defined at the data attribute level, which is input into the subprocesses.

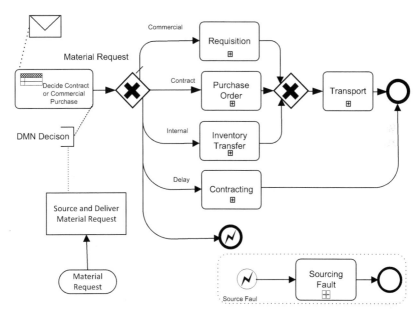

Figure 6.7 *The top-leveltop-level process and decision for the material sourcing decision.*

The activity of decision modeling uncovers a number of activity types. Often, decisions have two steps, one automatic and the next with human interventions. In the case of our top-level process and decision, some conditions will drive a human step, such as extending the terms of a contract. In addition, conditions and events that will generate errors, warning, and alerts will be discovered that the process should handle.

Exploring the detail of important decisions uncovers weaknesses and loose procedure. The process of creating documented decisions can strengthen these.

In these examples, these queries uncover weaknesses:

- What do we do if there is no decision?
- How do we defer to the contract office?

In all the relevant decisions, the decision aggregates around the questions that are asked and the allowable answers. Business knowledge as implemented by expressions is built on groups of rules that answer these questions.

Below the top-level decision, there are four critical sub-decisions: sources, transportation, insurance, and reporting. Two of these will be explored in some detail. The first is the source decision.

Source Decision

As with all decisions, the first thing that must be determined is the question. The source decision's question is:

How should we source the material requirement?

There are four possible answers for sourcing the material:

- Internal sources: supply the material from internal inventory
- Use an existing contract as the source
- Make a commercial purchase of the material from a certified vendor
- No source could be identified

To decide this, sub-decisions are included:

- Is the product available in inventory?
- What contracts are available for the material?
- What are the contract prices of the material?
- What are the certified vendors for the products for contract and commercial purchases?

These sub-decisions are shown in Figure 6.8. Contract sub-decisions will be further broken into more sub-decisions is a subsequent diagram.

As mentioned in the original presentation of the use cases, there are policies for contracting and commercial purchases. In addition, the top-level decision must select among competing sub-decisions.

Business Knowledge and Expressions for Contract Selection

As shown in Figure 6.9 below, the top decision is contract selection. If multiple contracts have been identified, then the contract selection policies are used to identify a single contract to use in our material sourcing decision. Typically, these policies are based on the lowest cost; however, minimum delivery clauses and supply diversity policies can affect this selection.

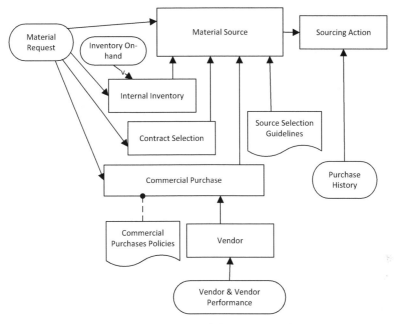

Figure 6.8 *The Material source decision and the relevant sub-decisions for the material sourcing.*

The contract selection decisions require a number of sub-decisions to complete. These are:

- Contract sourcing: What are the contracts that can meet the need in the material request?
- Contract status: Are contacts available from qualified vendors (another sub-decision) for this material request?
- Contract costs: If contracts are available, what are the costs?
- Contract actions: Are any contract actions needed for this contract?

Contract sourcing is a sub-decision whose question is:

What are the available contracts for this material requisition?

The answers to the question are:

- There are candidate contracts identified for this material requisition.
- There are contracts potentially available if contract actions are taken.
- There are no contracts that match this need.
- There are contract actions identified in this evaluation.

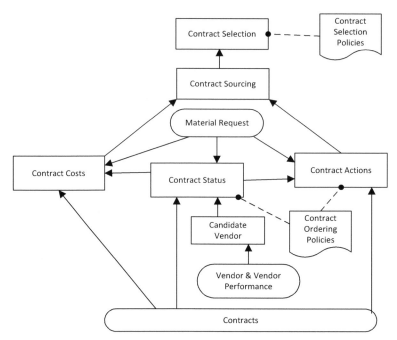

Figure 6.9 *Contract selection decision.*

For the contract selection business knowledge, these expressions are used:

- If the contract covers the requested material in the needed geographic service area, then the contract is applicable. To implement this expression, the following must be done: **Compare** the requested material with the available material in the contracts and the service area, and **Direct** the contract to be included in the candidate contracts.

- If the contract is set to end up to four days before the scheduled delivery date, then the contract is applicable. To implement this expression, the following must be done: **Compute** the difference between the contract expiration date and the shipment date, and **Compare** result with the redlined four, then **Direct** its inclusions in the Candidate Contract list if days is greater than four; or

- If the contract is set to end between four before and 21 days after the scheduled delivery date, then the contract is applicable with a contract action. To implement this expression, the following must be done: **Compute** the difference between the contract expiration date and the shipment date, and **Compare** the result with the redline greater than four and less than 21, then **Direct** a delay in the sourcing and its inclusions in the candidate contract.

- If the requested quantity plus the contract's total delivered-to date is greater than 90 percent of the contract's total maximum negotiated quantity, the contract is not applicable. To implement this expression, the following must be done: **Compute** the percentage difference between the total maximum negotiated quantity and the total delivered to date, plus the requested quantity, and **Compare** the computed value to the 90 percent threshold, then **Direct** to include in candidate contracts if the value is less than 90 percent.

- If the requested quantity plus the contract's total delivered-to date is between 90 percent and 120 percent of contract's total maximum negotiated quantity the contract is applicable with a contract action. To implement this expression, the following must be done: **Compute** the percentage difference between the total maximum negotiated quantity and the total delivered-to date, plus the requested quantity, and **Compare** the computed value to fall between the 90 percent and 120 percent threshold, then **Direct** to delay the sourcing on the material and include in candidate contracts if the value is greater than 90 percent and 120 percent.

Business Knowledge and Expressions for Contract Actions

The material requisition might need to identify the need to take actions with applicable contracts that are at threshold of contact policies. The expression for this is:

- If the candidate contract line item delivery total, plus the needed quantities, are between 90 percent and 120 percent, or if the contract is set to end between 4 before and 21 days after the scheduled delivery date, then Contract Manager is notified to investigate a contract extension. To implement this expression, we **Direct** that, if either of these previously conditions are true, then assign an output attribute with a value for the process to flag this warning event.

Business Knowledge and Expressions for Contract Costs

If there is a candidate contract available for a candidate vendor, then compute the cost of the contract. Contract cost is the unit cost of the material times the line item cost of the contract, less any discounts available.

Business Knowledge and Expressions for Candidate Vendor

The candidate vendor decision decides which supplier should be used. This is applicable for both the commercial purchase and the contract sourcing. This is equivalent to a black, white, and grey list. A supplier for either a contract or commercial purchase can be used if it can provide the material in the needed service area.

Based on the performance of the vendor's lab test, the process either rejects the candidate or obtains approval from the contract manager. The candidate vendor is rejected if it has four or more quality returns or eight bad lab tests within 90 days. This is an example of a "Yes, No, Maybe" decision table for filtering a list. This is shown as a decision table with rules as columns. Each row is a variable, and each column is a rule.

Vendor Qualification			
Lab Test Failure, 90 day	<8	>8	
Product Returns	<4	>4	
Inclusion as Candidate	Yes	No	Maybe
F	1	2	3

Figure 6.10 *Vendor inclusion rules as columns decision table.*

Business Knowledge and Expressions for Commercial Purchase

If there is a candidate vendor available for the material requisition, then the price of the product should be calculated. Commercial purchase cost is the unit cost of the material multiplied by the line item cost of the contract less any discounts available.

Business Knowledge and Expressions for Internal Inventory

This decision determines if there is there is on-hand inventory available. The inventory can be used if the material is available in the needed service area. To evaluate the expressions we **Compare** the requested material with the available material in on-hand inventory within the service area.

The on-hand cost is computed as the unit cost of the material multiplied by the line item internal cost of the material.

Business Knowledge and Expressions for Sourcing Action

As shown in Figure 6.8, the sourcing action actually follows the material sourcing action. Policies at the company decide when the contracting office should initiate a contract for purchasing material.

If more than $200,000 of a material in a region is purchased within a 12-month time frame, and there is no active contract for that material, then purchasing is directed to investigate contract solicitations. To implement this expression, **Compute** the value of the purchase of this type of material within 12 months, assign to total purchases, **Compare** the total purchase with the $200,000 threshold; then **Direct** if greater than $200,000, set attributes that will provide data for the contacting office to respond.

Business Knowledge and Expressions for Purchasing Policies

If several sources were found, such as contract and commercial, then the final criteria that must be accounted for are the added costs of commercial purchases and the benefits of internal inventory. Mature purchasing organizations favor a hierarchy of sourcing strategies, and they understand the costs involved. For instance, internal inventory is already acquired; there is no overhead associated. Contract purchases are preferred over commercial purchases because there is less administrative cost associated with contract purchases; the vendor has already agreed to the terms of the contracting organization.

In this use case, contract purchases over commercial purchases will be selected, even if they are 6 percent higher. Similarly, on-hand inventory will be accepted over any other alternate, even when it is 8 percent higher than the others.

First, the minimum price must be selected from the chosen sources by inspecting the prices that were located in the contract, commercial, and internal sources above.

Like the inspection results, lab tests, and product returns, the purchasing policies can be expressed as a decision table:

Source Selection				
Contact Price	<= minPrice*1.06			
Internal Inventory		<= minPrice*1.08		
Commercial			>0	
Selection	Contract	Inventory	Commercial	None
F	1	2	3	4

Figure 6.11 *Row-as-rule table with selection criteria for sources of material where contract and inventory prices are close to the commercial purchases price.*

If no source is found for the materials, then return selection 4: None –"no source identified" condition.

If the commercial purchase is not the minimum price, then select the source with the minimum price.

If the commercial purchase is the minimum price, then assign the source according to the rules in Figure 6.10.

Process Responses

At the top-level decision, the process responses were already determined:
Task sequencing process response (see Figure 6.5):

- Purchase order if contract is lowest cost source
- Requisition if commercial purchase is lowest cost source
- Transfer if on-hand inventory is lowest cost source

Actor inclusion (see Figure 6.4):

- Contract manager to review contract extension

Event identification & actor inclusions (see Figures 6.4 and 6.5):

- Purchasing to investigate more than $200,000 in material commercial purchases without a contract

These two new activities will now be added to the initial draft of the material request process:

Transportation Decision

Transportation is decided based on a combination of the lowest cost and the availability of insurance. The question for the transportation decision is:
How should the material be transported according to the needs of the material request and the insurance requirements of the enterprise?
The acceptable answers are:
There are seven choices for transportation:

- Internal (local) trucking
- Contract truck
- Carrier truck
- Contract rail
- Carrier rail
- Contract barge
- Carrier barge

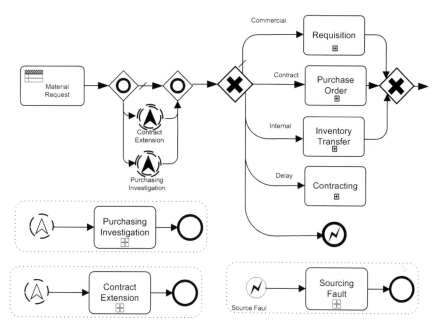

Figure 6.12 *The material source process with the two additional event subprocesses that arise from the source decision.*

There are several sub-decisions that are needed. The mode of shipment must be decided, as well as the availability of a contract line in the material delivery contract (FOB destination), the cost of a carrier, and the availability of insurance.

These sub-decisions are shown in the diagram below.

Transportation is decided based on the size of the material order and delivery sizes of the transport medium. Quotations for contract purchases can include transportation (FOB destination and FOB origin), and for this reason, the material source decision is a sub-decision for the transportation decision.

Another complex decision is transportation routing. Not every plant or contractor provides rail and water facilities, so these modes are often intermodal. In addition, facilities have different rates at which they can receive material into productive inventory. Transportation is generally routed using standard schedules. The transportation route includes the states, counties, and roads that are included on the route. However, realistically, unlike single mode transportation, multi-modal transportation will require human intervention to plan. If the decision is to use multi-mode transportation, an event subprocess can handle this.

At this point, every decision will not be expanded into business knowledge and expressions; however, the selection of transportation mode will be examined as an example of the use of a decision table with rows as rules.

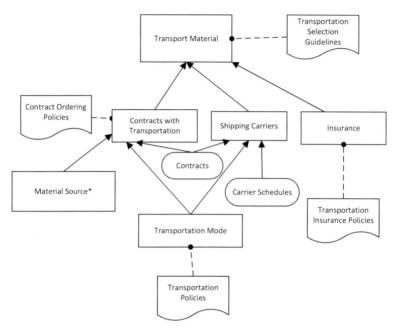

Figure 6.13 *In the transportation decision, the material source is a sub-decision.*

Business Knowledge and Expressions for Transportation Mode

The advantage of the larger bulk carriers is in the reduced number of shipments. At lower volumes or weight, rail and barge carriers are obviously not considered. In addition, there are limited numbers of materials that can be shipped by rail or barge. The modes of transportation are decided by the shipping weight (GWT) or shipment volume as shown in Figure 6.14.

- Expression: If the quality requested returns a value from Figure 6.9, then the transportation mode is a candidate mode.

The transportation modes feed into the contract, carrier, and insurance decisions.

Business Knowledge and Expressions for Local Transportation

In some cases, the small fleet of company transportation can provide shipping at an economical cost. Online quotations are obtained for commercial carriers of all other forms.

Transportation Mode			
F	Measure Value Lower Range	Units	Coverage
	>100	Ton	Rail
	>15,000	Lbs	Barge
	>30,000	Gallons	Rail
	>70,000	Gallons	Barge
			Trucking

Figure 6.14 *A decision table for the transportation modes.*

SUMMARY MATERIAL SOURCING PROCESSES

At the top level, the choice of the source of the material is combined with the transportation. If transportation is available on a contract and the FOB destination cost is the lowest, then transportation will be included in the contracting requisition. In addition, the transportation process is subsequent to the activities of requisitioning the material.

In this example, a single, comprehensive decision can drive an entire complex process without the need to perform many logic checks, and the process proceeds.

CONCLUSION

This chapter has shown how the BPMN in processes is affected by decisions in DMN. The result is to design processes that are in line with operational, compliance, and risk management objectives. Details of compliance include these elements:

- The sequence of a process' activities and events.
- Who is included in and assigned to a task.
- What course of action is taken.
- What data is valid.
- How to detect, control, and respond to events.

Process behavior considers decision-generated events which can be identified within the decision. As the use case shows, a single decision can trigger and control many aspects of business processes.

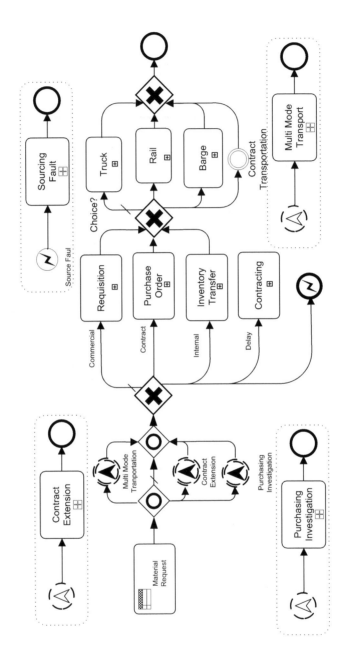

Figure 6.15 *The material request process with sourcing and transportation.*

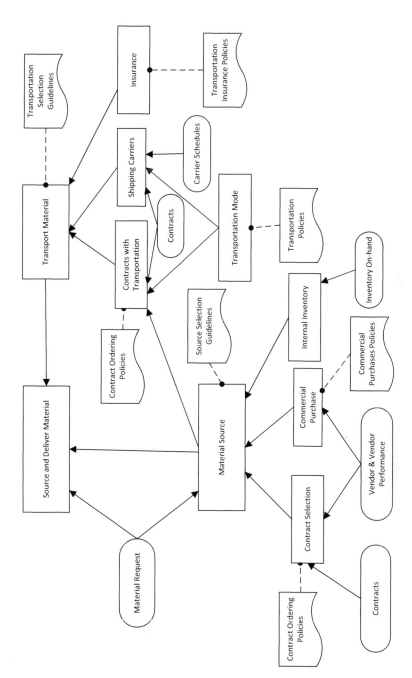

Figure 6.16 *The material request decision with the major sub-decisions shown.*

Five different ways that a decision's outcome can direct the pathways of the process were described. In the transportation example, the use case:

- Identified actors that needed to complete tasks, including the contract manager, the purchasing manager, and the transportation department.
- Identified the tasks that needed to be completed, including creating contracts for products that were excessively purchased commercially and renewing contracts.
- Identified the sequence of activities, as in the timely ordering of equipment.

As an organizing design idea, the process decision is both an important management concept and a strategic design tool for achieving business objectives and goals.

Well-designed processes simplify management control of business processes. In the absence of DMN, decisions are not separated from the business processes. This creates a weak model because decisions both change and control critical elements of the process.

Separating processes from decisions stabilizes business processes and permits change without having to change the process application. Understanding the five process compliance categories simplifies the choice of what should be dynamic decisions supported by expressions and what should be a static part of the process.

Both business processes and decisions are important intellectual assets that need to be documented, managed, and shared in BPMN/DMN. This can be achieved across the enterprise using repositories and software tools.

The use case explored, while missing many of the finer details, actually mirrors the practices of a mature enterprise. Contracts are used to aggregate the favorable purchasing power. All of the factors of the decision are considered, including transportation, insurance, and environmental reporting. The central point of the exercise is to simulate the complexity of a real-life scenario.

Here are the key components of the BPMN/DMN approach:

- Business processes and decisions should be model-driven and visual.
- Teams need tools that analyze, model, and test the impact of changes to business processes and decisions across the enterprise.
- Organizations seek to trace decisions to policy and organization objectives.

In summary, from the perspective of governance, risk, and compliance, the five process responses define a critical part of the process.

CHAPTER 7

EXECUTION SEMANTICS

INTRODUCTION

BPMN and DMN are employed to depict process scenarios and use cases in a manner that business analysts can understand. Yet to become a digitized, executable process, the business details of the process model must become a technical deliverable. For example, in a purchasing use case:

- The period of performance for a contract becomes two data elements populated from the query of a Representational State Transfer (REST) service.
- A demographics web form is created at the point of the user task.
- A six-month projection of inventory demand becomes a regression against an array of numbers.
- A sequence of contract conditions becomes FEEL logic.

But even describing the placement of these with proper BPMN activities, events, gateways, transitions, and messages, and with the proper applications of decision-oriented modeling and workflow patterns, no BPMN/DMN tool can guarantee the execution-ready state of the process. Obviously, even when the process is syntactically correct, more modeling work remains. In some cases, additional detailed analysis of the model must be applied. In other cases, elements must be adjusted to ones that are recognized by the execution engine. Additionally, the process model must accommodate the true nature of the technical characteristics of the interactions with the infrastructure.

First, to be considered execution-worthy, the full picture of the process model should be completed. The happy path must be detailed with exceptions, escalations, and compensations. Some of the BPMN patterns for managing these were covered in Chapter 5. Frequently, these more complex details can obscure the intent of the process from the business community—it is not always obvious when an event subprocess is started. Here the modeling team might consider maintaining separate models. Also, there are points at which processes become so unwieldy that they obscure the fundamental business nature of the process. For instance, Chapter 5 covered more complex scenarios in event processing.

Next, the nature of the execution semantics of the model, as described in Chapter 14 of OMG's BPMN 2.0 Specification, should be evaluated against the intended nature of the process. Execution semantics accurately prescribes how a proper BPMN engine will interpret the configuration of model elements. This description is not just the functioning of gateways and conduct of activities; there are important characteristics that connect elements of the BPMN data model with the engine. Chapter 3 reviewed the data object and the message specification.

The conforming engine launches process instances and controls their internal states precisely as they are described by these semantics. There are BPMN elements that can be optionally ignored by the engine. These include manual and abstract tasks, ad hoc processes, and others. The modeling team should become familiar with specifics of the target engine in this area.

The specification's execution semantics uses the token concept. Tokens traverse the sequence flows and pass through the BPMN. For some elements, especially gateways and implicit splits and merges, the execution semantics describes how the token defines the behavior of an executing process.

In most cases, the semantics of a category of elements is hierarchical. A looping subprocess inherits the semantics of the subprocess; a script or service activity inherits the semantics of the activity. Further, there are important aspects of the BPMN's XML data model that are critical for understanding what elements do. That said, most of the elements should be clear to practitioners. For example, exclusive gateways have conditions, subprocesses have input and output data sets and multi-instance subprocesses have counts.

COMPLETING THE PROCESS MODEL FOR EXECUTION

To complete a BPMN model, anticipated exceptions must be accommodated by either:

- Catching events at the boundary of the subprocess and directing them to activities that can correct, waiting for an alleviation of the constraint, or trapping the condition.
- Adding an error condition to gateways that directs anticipated errors.
- Referencing a standard subprocess at the escalation of any error.

These exceptions are determined by the business problem that is being solved, the nature of the internal and external services that are being connected, and the characteristics of the infrastructure that hosts the executable services. In addition, next to optimizing a process efficiently, managing exceptions is one of the clear benefits of the business process approach.

For example, in the BPMN fragments below, an error checking message is passed through a device cloud[1] interface to a device on a cellular network that might be offline for various reasons.

Here, in the earlier phases of modeling, a happy path level of effort was completed, and now that the model is to be executable, exceptions must be accommodated. Business and technical exceptions can occur here. For instance:

- In business exceptions, a device might not have been properly commissioned, and a special exception process might need to be started.
- In technical exceptions, security equipment might detect a man-in-the middle attack.

These possible errors should be handled and might entail the modeling of additional workflows.

As mentioned earlier, the execution semantics of BPMN normally preclude the use of abstract tasks. So, abstract tasks (not shown in Figure 7.1) should be replaced with scripts, services, and human tasks. Message tasks might be replaced with service calls or scripts where possible:

- A service task can communicate with other processes and services. In execution, the service task is used when a process must invoke an external service or process. Typically, this denotes a call to Web Service Definition Language (WSDL) or RESTful services.
- The script task manipulates the values of data objects within the process. Typically, a gateway might direct the flow of the process. The script task is used to denote this change in the business process. For example, you might set the default or look up values of data objects at the start of a process.

For example, Figure 7.1's message to and from the device cloud will require analysis in the execution phase. These services generally occur across four layers of infrastructure: the corporate Software as a Service (SaaS), where user applications are hosted, a device cloud, a computing gateway, and a network or grid of connected sensors and devices. Communications at the first layer from the SaaS platform are generally performed over HTTP to REST services, hiding the details of the actual message. Communication from the device cloud to the devices is fre-

---

1. A device cloud is a Platform as a Service (PaaS) that is usually hosted by a third party that commissions, provisions, and communicates with the IoT devices. IoT solutions often involve millions of devices with many types of device profiles.

quently done with a message queue such as MQ Telemetry Transport (MQTT)[1]. While the device cloud hides the complexity of the queue, the exceptions that they handle should be reflected in the exceptions of the process that calls the REST services.

(Device Cloud)

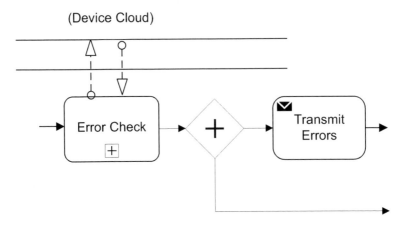

Figure 7.1 *An analytical representation of communications to devices in the device cloud through an error checking subprocess.*

The fragment from Figure 7.1 might require exceptions for error and time-out handling to execute. The nature of the error or time-out dictates the nature of the response. As shown in Figure 7.2, errors can often be corrected or ignored/noted and an activity restarted. In other cases, the activity can be skipped entirely. All these possibilities are easily modeled in BPMN.

In developing the proper tasks for the execution model, modelers first examine the operating characteristics of each task and select the appropriate type. As mentioned earlier, abstract tasks do not execute in BPMN. The executing tasks are selected for their implementation characteristics. For instance:

- The transmit error values uses an enterprise email server, and the original analyst's level message only depicted a one-way message.
- The evaluate communications error uses a rule shape because it decides what must be done with the stack of errors from the device.
- The handle time error task uses a script because it transforms the values of the time for the next execution.
- The device error data object is needed to hold the values created by the process instance.

---

1. MQTT is a machine-to-machine (M2M)/"Internet of Things" connectivity protocol. See MQTT.org for more information.

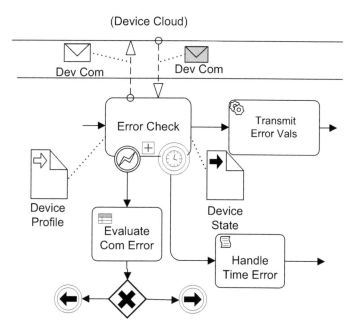

Figure 7.2 *As error handles are added to the analytical model, there are more considerations that must accommodate the realities of the technical infrastructure and the intent of the process.*

As this discussion illustrates, deciding what error or exceptions to trap is a matter of mastery of the details of the infrastructure where the executing process resides. For example, legacy database environments might experience a number of correctable exceptions that are not experienced in the same manner as in modern cloud environments. It is a best practice to provide for a generalized exception, including reusable subprocesses that trap a broad set of unplanned conditions. These might be managed in an Information Technology Infrastructure Library (ITIL) manner and modeled as event subprocesses. Still, interfaces to external entities, partners, and companies that do not provide service level agreements (SLAs) should be managed accordingly.

Tasks for Model Execution

Table 7.1 presents some of the conditions and design scenarios that might indicate the replacement of an abstract or another task with a more specific task that follows the execution semantics of BPMN. The table also illustrates how the specification prescribes task execution and completion for the different task types. It is important to match the system's operational characteristics with the proper task type.

Table 7.1 Replacements, Corrections, and Variations in BPMN Models

Shape	Example Usage	Design Scenario	Sample Execution Semantic
Script Task	Change values of data objects at the point of a process or change the values of data objects outside of another flow object. This is typically done in a programming language such as Xpath, Jscript, or Visual Basic(.net).	Populate a complex business object from data input into a process. Transform one business object into another.	Upon instantiation, the associated script is invoked. Upon completion, the task is marked completed.
Service Task	Analogous to message send and receive tasks or the event messages throw and catch; however, synchronously invokes processes and services. With this task, the process waits at the service task until a response is returned.	A message queue when the response is immediately expected. An email sent to an enterprise mail server. A message on a JMS pipe.	The service is called upon instantiation. If the service fails, the activity is marked as failure.
User Task	Process participants interact with forms of various types. The user interface include the widgets, field prompts that process participants see, are populate with the tasks.	Web screens, mobile applications that are placed on a task list.	Upon instantiation, the User Task is distributed to the assigned person or group of people.
Rule Task	Denotes the call of a business rules management system to make a decision.	Apply business rules defined in a decision model and so make a choice or selection that impacts process execution.	Upon instantiation, the associated decision model is executed.

Table 7.1 Replacements, Corrections, and Variations in BPMN Models (cont'd)

Shape	Example Usage	Design Scenario	Sample Execution Semantic
Message Task (Receive) / Message Task (Send)	Where asynchronous throwing and catching is needed to coordinate activities.	Process the outcome of a participant's activity.	Upon instantiation, the associated Message is sent, and the Send Task completes. If the task is a type, the Receive task waits for the message to arrive. When the message arrives, the Receive task completes.

Each task type is a type of activity that can be executed by a process engine. All activities share common attributes and behavior, such as states and state transitions. The BPMN 2.0 specification defines how the activities must move from instantiation through the potentials for interruption, compensation, or termination, if applicable. The outcome is that the process engine might mark the activity as completed, failed, compensated, terminated, or withdrawn.

The intent of the BPMN 2.0 designers with respect to the different task shapes is clearer when they are considered as notation that describes their execution.

Synchronous and Asynchronous Service Calls

In BPMN models, there are patterns for synchronous and asynchronous communications. In the service call for transmitting error values in Figure 7.2, the answering message arrives synchronously. If a response arrives later, the communication is asynchronous. Message events commonly represent asynchronous communications.

Yet not only should the nature of the interfaces to systems be understood, as in the case of the message queuing for the device cloud, but the synchronicity of the process also must be coordinated with activities. Processes request important services and must wait for their completion:

- Inspection of materials in supply chains often need certified lab results.
- Customers provide critical information for loan applications.
- Supply chain partners provide finished goods and services.

The process that orchestrates these must interact with the requested service in the proper way. When developing deeper understanding for execution, modelers make adjustments to the sequence of activities so that services are either synchronously or asynchronously gathered.

There are two aspects to these scenarios. Although the communications appears asynchronous at the business level, the APIs to these services might be technically synchronous services.

In an asynchronous service, the answer to a request can be delayed. This can present a time window for other process work to be performed. In a synchronous service, the sender waits for a response. The response should be rapid on a process time scale; however, there are circumstances where the wait is unpredictable. This applies to human and system participants alike.

Synchronous communication is simple: a response is returned directly in an application interface. Asynchronous styles are more complex because delayed responses must be assigned to the waiting process instance. This is known as defining a *correlation condition*. The BPMN specification describes how messages need to reach a specific process instance with a correlation to identify the particular instance.

Both synchronous and asynchronous communications must be able to locate the target of the message using correlations. A *correlation* is the connection of an event or message with process instances. Designers need to properly define the correlation so the process engine can assign incoming messages to the correct process instances. The execution semantics of instance routing prescribe the creation of a correlation key as an expression.

There are a number of correlation approaches to building the correlation key(s). First, there is the pure, key-based approach: a data key value is generated for conversations, and the key is used in call and response messages. The process engine correlates the messages with the key. Key-based approaches can also use business attributes such as order numbers. The semantics allow the expression to build the key on the fly with the technical expressions (correlation property retrieval expression) that define how to find these properties in the process variables or incoming messages. The second approach is a subscription or context-based correlation. It is built atop the key-based approach. At runtime, the correlation key instance holds a composite key that is dynamically calculated and updated whenever the underlying data objects or properties change.

DATA MODELING

In addition to completing the process model, the data elements for the process instance must be defined and added to the diagram at the points of input, output, message flows, and storage. Chapter 4 discussed the data object, persistent storage and messages, and how these artifacts can detail an executable model.

Data is critical for creating transaction information; it is a crucial source of information for decisions and process payloads. In the process diagram, the input of data was defined as the device profile, and the device error is represented as an output data object. The attributes of the data object are developed with traditional data modeling; however, neither BPMN nor DMN depict a data model. BPMN connects a data model to activities, while DMN connects it to input data. Data is accommodated as XML schemas in various technologies. The data definition from the modeling effort can be merged directly into XML code.

Data sets are critical for activities. In the semantics of the activities above, an input dataset must be available for activities to enter an active state. An input set is available if each of its required data inputs is available. Activities wait until the data becomes available. Similarly, output datasets, upon completion, are checked for availability and completion. If no data is output, an error is thrown.

Data Object

The objective of the data object in BPMN is to document the inputs and outputs of process activities and connect a schema's data objects with the inputs and outputs of the activity. The data object is a rectangle with the upper right corner folded over, as shown here:

Purchase Order

The text label for a data object is underneath the shape. Often, the current state of the data object is shown in brackets under the text label. As the diagram progresses, the state of the data object can easily be read, as displayed in Figure 7.3.

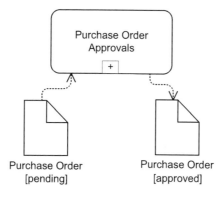

Purchase Order [pending]   Purchase Order [approved]

Figure 7.3 *Use of data objects shapes.*

As with the text annotation, the association line connects the data artifact to another shape. Data object shapes are often associated with tasks, gateways, events, sequence lines, or message lines. In message flow, data objects portray the payload or content of messages.

A data object can be associated with an activity, which signifies where the data is produced. Associating data artifacts with a gateway can show the data upon which a decision is based.

Data modeling is as critical as process, decision, and event modeling. A data object is a visual depiction of the modeled subject or business entity. A data model may depict an electronic form or a physical document. Data objects provide information about what activities need to be performed and/or what they produce. For instance, an inventory manager might requisition special items. The requisition would be a data item. Input and output data is a formal part of the BPMN 2.0 specification and affects execution.

In some cases, the data object denotes a collection of a data type. It uses the same base shape but adds the multiplicity symbol, three vertical bars. For example, a set of contract documents could be illustrated with the collection symbol.

Contract Documents

The data objects can show direction of document flow. For example, are the contracts an input to the "Legal Approval" activity or are they an output? This can be accomplished in several ways. First, the annotation association lines can have an arrow pointing to the direction of flow, as in Figure 7.4.

The data object shape allows for additional annotation (an arrow) showing whether or the data elements are being sent (output) or received (input). Similar to the event shapes, the white (empty) arrow means "receive," and the black (filled) arrow means "send." Figure 7.4 shows how these shapes are used and how they can add detail to a diagram.

The input and output annotations on the data objects can also be used in conjunction with the collection symbol. Therefore, there are six types of data object shapes, as seen in Figure 7.5.

Input data object types provide detail to the activities of the process. An input or output data object references a schema element and creates the input and output specification. When developing an executable process, an element is noted within a schema in XML and can be referenced by the data object. The specification of the input and output models the data behavior of the process.

Boolean conditions in gateways can also reference the data elements.

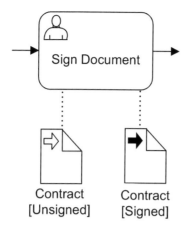

Figure 7.4 *Data objects as inputs and outputs to activity.*

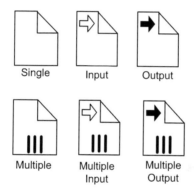

Figure 7.5 *Table of data object types.*

Data Stores

The data store artifact shown in Figure 7.6 is similar to a database symbol used in modeling notations other than BPMN. The data store is a concept that represents a permanent place for data storage. For the analyst, the important detail is the data associated with permanent storage. The data is not transient; it is persistent. Simple data objects are not.

Figure 7.6 *BPMN for Data Store.*

The data store inherits all the data that is associated with the flow. This clearly indicates that the data is available to other people and systems outside of the process.

The Data source artifacts in Figure 7.7 illustrate the proper use of this shape. This process interfaces with an IT business process.

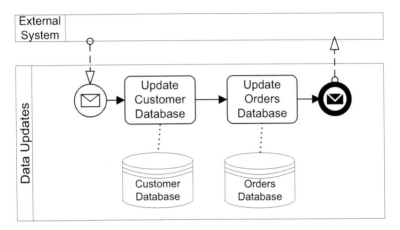

Figure 7.7 *Data source artifact used to denote persistent storage.*

Message

BPMN provides two message shapes for use as data detail. The message shape is the same envelope-like shape that is used inside a message event, and there are two forms of the message: a white shape for a message that initiates a process, and a lightly filled message for non-initiating messages. The two messages are shown below:

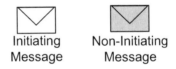

Message artifacts can be associated with any activity, event, or messaging flow. They cannot be associated with gateways or sequence flow. The direction of message flow can be shown by associating the shape with a message flow line.

As a process is modeled for the purpose of execution, the message becomes more important. Message flows need to be sufficiently detailed to permit alignment of participants and callable processes. Messages reference a data type according to the item definition in the associated schema.

Figure 7.8 shows the usage of the message shape. The association lines (dotted) are used to create the relationship between the message and where the message is used. When the manager in Figure 7.8 sends a work request message, it is received as a process start event. This is an initiating message, so the envelope is white. The response task is in the work queue of the worker. When the worker begins the task, it becomes active. After the task is completed, the send notification event occurs, which sends the completion notification message. The completion message is shown as a non-initiating message with light shading.

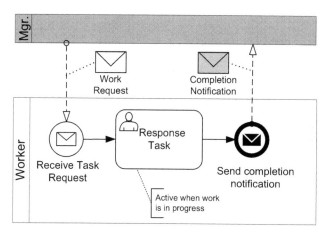

Figure 7.8 *Message artifact shape usage.*

EXECUTION SEMANTICS

Execution semantics precisely define how the BPMN 2.0 specification expects an engine to translate the structure of a valid BPMN diagram into process instances that are started, stopped, and cancelled. They also define how activities and events are interpreted. There are two primary concepts that explain how the engine executes the process model, process instance, and the Token Passing Model.

A process engine generally assigns a computer server's resources to a process instance. These resources include one or more threads, CPU memory, disk space, and perhaps utilities for parallelism, hardening, and fail-over. On top of all this, there is a unique identifier associated with the process instance. The BPMS tool will use this identifier so it can internally correlate messaging and track the state of data variables in their various scopes. Generally, there is a process instance for each iteration of a process: one per customer order or per insurance claim. However, there are some cases where a single process instance might be used to monitor events or as an overseer.

Within the running instance, the token is a tool for modeling and understanding the behavior of the internal sequence flow of processes, particularly at sequences and transitions, both implicit merges and joins and at gateways. Process semantics describe how BPMN elements interact with tokens as they flow across the sequences of elements of the process instance. Once token passing is understood, many of the semantics of execution are self-apparent. The definition of the shape describes how the engine is expected to execute the orchestration of activities. For instance, as was mentioned in Chapter 2, parallel and inclusive gateways create and consume multiple tokens, and exclusive elements create and consume a single token.

Implicit Splits and Merges

By convention, a multi-split can be equated to an explicit parallel split. When there are three or more sequences leaving, a combination of conditions can apply. First, when there are multiple outgoing, unconditional sequence flows, they behave like a single parallel gateway split. As shown in Figure 7.9 below, multiple outgoing sequences with conditions behave like an inclusive split. A mix of multiple outgoing sequences with and without conditions is considered as a combination of a parallel and an inclusive split.

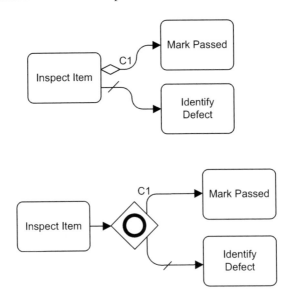

Figure 7.9 *These two BPMN fragments are equivalent because two outgoing sequences with conditions behave like an inclusive split.*

As shown in Figure 7.10 below, there is a convention for multiple incoming flows. Similarly for implicit joins, called uncontrolled flow in the specification, the presence of multiple incoming sequences behaves as an exclusive gateway. To eliminate the ambiguity of these conditions, it is suggested that gateways (other than exclusive) should be explicitly included in the process flow. In fact, even the exclusive gateway should be used so that diagrams are easier to understand.

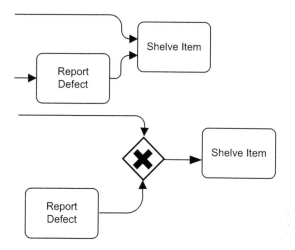

Figure 7.10 *These two BPMN fragments are equivalent because two incoming sequences behave like a data-based exclusive merge.*

In the process of moving an analytical model to execution, implicit splits and merges should be examined for their conformance to the expected business model. Since multiple merges behave as a data-based inclusive merge, it is common practice to use this in models. Yet assumptions can change over time, and additional details can be placed on the process model that alters the original.

Understanding the Execution Semantics of the Gateways

The combination of the token passing model and the semantics on parallel, inclusive, and exclusive splits and merges defines the universe of how BPMN expects activities and events to be orchestrated within a process. Table 7.2 summarizes the semantics of the gateways and the nature of the merging and splitting of flows after the elements.

In execution semantics, parallel execution means that the engine executes the process token on a parallel thread. This is true for parallel, inclusive, and complex gateways. This can be an advantage to clustered environments and massively parallel server environments.

Chapter 4 covered the complex gateway in detail. The complex gateway was, in part, an attempt to model the dead path elimination capabilities of Business Process Execution Language (BPEL). To accomplish this, complex gateways enable a process to synchronize N paths from M incoming transitions ($N <= M$). With the complex gateway, parallel (or inclusive) branches converge, and outbound

Table 7.2 Execution Semantics for BPMN Gateways

Gateway Type	Inbound-Merging Behavior	Shape Graphic	Outbound-Sequence Splitting Behavior	Operational Semantics
Parallel Gateway (Fork and Join)	Synchronize multiple concurrent branches, e.g., wait until all arrive.		Spawn new concurrent threads on parallel branches, each get a token.	Activated when one token at each incoming sequence, produces exactly one token and concurrent thread at each outflow.
Exclusive Gateway (Exclusive Decision [data-based] and Exclusive Merge)	Pass-through for a set of incoming branches.		Activation of exactly one out outgoing branch.	The first, true condition determines the sequence for the token, and no other conditions are evaluated. If none true, the default branch is taken. Exception is thrown when none is evaluated.
Inclusive Gateway (Inclusive Decision and Inclusive Merge)	Synchronizes true branches of concurrent incoming branches, waits for the true tokens to arrive.		Spawn new concurrent threads (with a token) on parallel branches that have conditions that are true.	The Inclusive Gateway is activated if all incoming sequences with tokens have arrived. All conditions that evaluate to true create a thread and token, unless none are true; then the default is taken. Exception is thrown when none is evaluated.
Event-Based Gateway (Exclusive Decision [event-based])	Pass-through semantics for incoming branches.		Exactly one of the outgoing branches (with the triggered event) is activated afterwards.	When used at the process start as a Parallel Event Gateway, only message-based triggers are allowed.

Table 7.2 Execution Semantics for BPMN Gateways (cont'd)

Complex Gateway (related to Complex Condition and Complex Merge)	Complex synchronization behavior, in particular, race situations.		Each has a Boolean operator that determines what sequence receives a token.	See discussion below.

activity is activated once the incoming branches are complete. The result of the rest of the *M* minus *N* branches is ignored. Execution is blocked until the *M* incoming branches have been triggered and unblocked when their execution is completed.

Understanding the Life of the Instance

A process is instantiated when one of its Start Events occurs. BPMN specifies seven types of start events: none, message, timer, conditional, single, multiple, and multiple parallel. In conventional orchestration, each occurrence of one of these creates a new process instance and one or more tokens. In a process engine the instance is generally identified by a key and the instance data

In process thinking, an instance of a process accomplishes an objective, and the instance is uniquely identified by the process engine. In BPMN, instances are started by implicit or explicit start events.

Start Events

A start event begins or instantiates a process. Explicit and implicit start events will each create a new process instance, unless the start event is an element of a conversation among other start events. The start event is the origin of the initial tokens in a process flow. The instance is a critical concept in BPM. It has its own identity and scope.

There are many considerations with managing processes in an infrastructure. Simple (empty) starts are generally used for governing and monitoring processes, and these can be critical to the integrity of the process ecosystem. Large systems must coexist with system monitors such as Tivoli and HP OpenView; BPM must coordinate and centralize operations, as these communicate with messaging buses. Empty starts are not generally used; however, the execution semantics imply that the process should start when the BPM server is started.

As mentioned before, the event-based gateway can also start processes. In fact, multiple groups of event-based gateways can start a process, provided they share the same correlation information.

Intermediate Events

The semantics of the intermediate events call for waiting for the event to occur. Waiting starts when the specified point is reached. After the event occurs, it is consumed, and sequence flow continues.

End Events

End events can consume the final token of the process. If there are other tokens, then the end event cannot occur. Unless the event is a terminate event, the action completes the activity or subprocess normally and executes the action of the end event type. The completed process state drives many subsequent semantics.

Event Subprocess

As discussed in Chapter 4, event subprocesses were a major change to the BPMN specification. Starting elements for the event subprocess have all the characteristics of an event followed by a sequence of tasks and events. As shown in Figure 7.11 below, the starting event can be interrupting (a solid line circle) or non-interrupting (a dotted line circle). Event subprocesses are located within processes or subprocesses and are called out by dotted-line frames. The specification also allows the dotted line to be collapsed with the [+] notation.

As mentioned earlier, the process of defining a standard set of exceptions processes can be implemented as an event process. These can be important for creating standard responses to infrastructure errors/ITIL. For instance, in the example in Figure 7.11, a generalized error subprocess handles errors. This can be added throughout the execution system to standardize the response to unhandled exceptions in the process.

The execution semantics of the event subprocess follow from the characteristics of the starting event. While the enclosing process or subprocess is active, the non-interrupting event will trigger the event subprocess. The interrupting event subprocess will cancel the enclosing subprocess. Non-interrupting event subprocesses can be triggered as frequently as needed, as long as the process or subprocess remains active.

Semantically, the event subprocess:

- Can have incoming or outgoing sequence flow.
- The event is started by a trigger. There are seven triggers in BPMN semantics: message, error, escalation, compensation, conditional, signal, and multiple.

Execution Semantics for Subprocess

As processes are modeled, designers often use the subprocess to create high-level process models. There are five different subprocess types that are used here: the

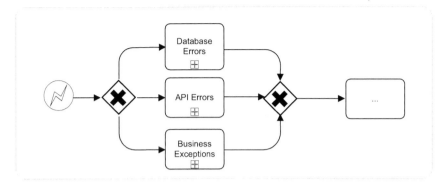

Figure 7.11 *An event subprocess for managing error exceptions.*

subprocess/call activity, the looping subprocess, the ad hoc sub process, the multi-instance subprocess, and the compensation subprocess.

A subprocess encapsulates a process and an activity, modeled by inner elements of activities, gateways, events and sequence flow. Once a subprocess is instantiated, it acts and behaves like a normal process. Most process engines identify the subprocess separately and can display statistics and data. The instantiation and completion of these vary by the type. Table 7.3 presents the execution semantics for all the subprocess types in BPMN.

Table 7.3 Execution Semantics for the Types of BPMN Subprocesses

Shape	Execution Usage	Design Scenario	Execution Semantic
Subprocess +	Abstract an objective that has a number of courses of actions in a high level diagram.	Identifiable objectives within a process. For example, a contract award subprocess would require a number of steps in a mature organization.	Started by a flow token, the sole empty start event gets a token upon instantiation; activities and gateways without incoming sequence flow get a token, a thread is instantiated for each start event that flows from outside, complete when all tokens consumed.

Table 7.3 Execution Semantics for the Types of BPMN Subprocesses (cont'd)

Looping Subprocess ↺ ⊞	Execute a process against a list or a set. Acts as a wrapper for an inner activity that can be executed multiple times in sequence.	For instance, loop through a list of business objects, invoice details or customers. All standard notions of looping are supported, e.g., for, while, until.	The same as the subprocess semantics, executes the inner activity as long as the loop condition evaluates to true. The test before attribute decides when the loop condition is evaluated. The loop maximum attribute bound the iteration that can be unbounded when unset. As with any subprocess, when the activities are complete and the condition is met, a token is generated for the outgoing sequence.
Multi-Sequential Subprocess ☰ ➕	Launch a set of sequential tasks that acts as a wrapper for an activity which has multiple instances spawned sequentially.	For processing in sequence, where resources might be constrained by the resource sizes.	The number of instances to be generated is evaluated once. There is a completion condition that is evaluated once an instance completes, when true the remaining instances are completed, and a token is generated. There is a behavior attribute that defines when instances can throw events.
Multi-Parallel Subprocess ||| ➕	Launch a set of sequential tasks, that acts as a wrapper for an activity which has multiple instances spawned in parallel or sequentially.	Activities that might need to use multiple resources to manage loads, queuing channels.	The same as the sequential subprocess except the inner activities are executed in sequence.

Table 7.3 Execution Semantics for the Types of BPMN Subprocesses (cont'd)

Ad-Hoc Subprocess ~ +	Human-selected sequence of related activities.	Unordered list of tasks required to complete an activity.	Activities within the ad hoc subprocess are not all connected by sequences; intermediate events must have outflowing sequence. Upon execution, all activities that have no incoming sequence are enabled. If parallel, another enabled activity can be selected for execution. This is not sequential .
Compen- sation ◁◁ +	A compensation handler is a set of activities not connected to other portions of the BPMN model.	Transaction and database records are written that must be removed because a portion on a subprocess was not completed.	Parent activity must be completed. When triggered, the subprocess is run and scope of original activity is restored for reversing the actions of parent. Compensations are performed in the reverse order of the process, according to the type of subprocess that is compensated.

Threads or process instances can consume many resources. If, during the business analysis design period, a subprocess was identified that only needs a limited numbers of activities or gateways to complete, the modeler might consider eliminating the subprocess and moving the activities outside the subprocess boundary. Another consideration that can retain the subprocess is the need for a separate enclosing scope.

Compensations

Compensations reverse steps (e.g., activities, database records) that were already completed because their results need to be reversed. Active items cannot be compensated but rather need to be canceled. An outcome of cancellation can be compensation of already completed activities.

Compensation is performed by a compensation handler. This can either be an event subprocess (for a subprocess or process) or an associated compensation activity (for any activity). Examples of these were presented at the end of Chapter 3. In the case of a subprocess, its compensation event subprocess has access to the parent subprocess data at the time of its completion, known as snapshot data.

Compensation is triggered by a throw compensation event (usually an error handler), a part of a cancellation, or another compensation handler. This event also specifies the activity for compensation. There can be a hierarchy or nested hierarchy of compensations. The order of the compensation is reversed to the extent that the subprocess type permits.

SUMMARY

Moving a process into execution can be an extensive effort and requires a precise understanding of not only BPMN but the nature of the environment, systems, and workflows. From this discussion, the steps needed to complete this activity can be discerned. These include:

- Completing the happy path by adding error, exception, escalation, and compensation handlers.
- Creating process data models, integrating other data modeling efforts, and specifying needed inputs, outputs, messages, and data stores.
- Gathering and developing an understanding of the nature of the systems and interfaces at the edges of the model and adjusting synchronous and asynchronous strategies.
- Developing a standard approach to handling exceptions and errors; considering creating a standard event-driven subprocess.
- Tracing the tokens across the final model; correcting the sequences of the path according to diversions from the needed behavior.

CHAPTER 8

CONCLUSIONS

This book has presented two ways of modeling the critical structural elements of an enterprise: the operational processes and the decisions that direct them. Both possess distinctly different characteristics. Business processes models describe a sequence of activities and the events, exceptions, and escalations that are necessary to execute them in the real word. Decisions are a network of sub-decisions that act on data guided by business knowledge. Together, they accurately and fully describe how processes operate.

Businesses have described their processes with flow charts since the 1930s. The workflow diagrams of the 1960s spawned from these, and legacy flow chart and workflow diagramming approaches are still in widespread use. However, the processes described by flow charts are high-level and generally do not reflect current approaches to business processes—the output of the workflow flows from functional area to functional area in a "batch" mode. A modern business process might describe the life cycle of an asset, such as a truck or factory robot, rather than describing the workflow mission of the maintenance or manufacturing division where the assets are an input. Modeling business processes with BPMN changes the focus from macro-level organization to more atomic objectives or goals. It also can handle much more than the happy path.

BPMN has evolved from these diagram types and has some shapes in common, but a BPMN process diagram represents a new way of thinking about a process. With BPMN, processes are mapped along a time continuum, imagining what activities can occur in sequence and in parallel and what gateways transition this. Process modelers also create and respond to business events and must decide how the business can gracefully recover from exceptions in a real-world process, which is the central purpose of the token concept. BPMN documents who performs the tasks, in what order, in what timeframe, and how these tasks interact with activities performed by other participants. The token concept models parallelism and deadlocking within this process.

BPMN has helped many organizations transition from functional to process-focused. BPMN alone offers improved models over workflow diagramming. However, when BPMN was first adopted, some challenges remained. Decisions, whether they were manual or automated using business rules management systems, were poorly defined. Sometimes, they were glossed over or the process was overcomplicated by additional process elements used to describe the decision making. Attempts to integrate business rules and business process often floundered, with individual activities that had to be mapped to hundreds or thousands of business rules. Process logic was confused with decision logic. Analytics were increasingly applied to the process and to its execution history but could not easily be applied within the process to route, assign, or act differently based on the analysis results.

Combining decision modeling in DMN and process modeling in BPMN addresses these challenges. With decisions called out and modeled explicitly, it is clear where business rules and analytics can be applied to make those decisions. Modeling decisions separately simplifies processes and allows for more effective event handling. The balance between manual and automated decision making clearly can be seen and managed. With BPMN and DMN, processes and decisions can be modeled as peers.

Decision modeling with DMN did not arrive out of nowhere. It, too, has evolved, primarily from earlier attempts to structure rules-based processing. These approaches were developed as it became clear that a rules-first approach to using business rules management systems could result in overly complex, over-connected business rules that were difficult to manage. Decision tables have long been a favored way to represent tabular business rules, and here too, the power of a network, of connecting decision tables or rule families into dependency networks, became clear. In parallel, those combining business rules with advanced analytics started developing approaches to effectively combine them. When the OMG brought these threads together, DMN was the result.

Decision modeling in DMN represents an entirely different mode of thinking from process modeling. There is no time element, and a decision is the total of sub-decisions, fed with input data and using business knowledge to evaluate expression and decision tables. With DMN, well-formed questions and answers are built, and modelers think in terms of the topology of the decision: the hierarchy of sub-decisions that feed into the central questions. Business rules can be defined, primarily as decision tables, to precisely specify how each sub-decision should be made. In addition, predictive analytic models can be incorporated into decision models, perhaps in the form of PMML, to allow for data-driven decision making. The output of the decision is created by assigning values to the output data. These decision results can then be used and consumed in the processes created.

Event analysis is the third critical area of business process modeling. This develops support for the decision-based processing of enterprise-significant events. Increasingly, it is also an essential part of strategy for applying data analytics within the context of the decision model and the evolving IoT. It is a crucial aspect of modern architectures in High Consequence Systems Architectures, including Command and Control applications like situational awareness.

To connect DMN and BPMN, business rule activity and the output data becomes the connector. There are several connection points within the OMG standards that describe the connection. First, DMN can use a specified schema for inputs and outputs. This schema can be aligned with the data objects in BPMN, which allows the output to direct the receiving process on how to comply with the decision. Secondly, metadata within a DMN model can specify which processes and activities use the decision.

As detailed in Chapter 6, decisions generally create five different outcomes that govern and control business operations. Decisions direct the:

- Order or sequence of a process' tasks, decisions, and internal events;
- Selection of who is included in and assigned to a task;
- Selection of the course of action;
- Selection of what is to be retained, its validity, and duration; and
- Detection, control, and responses to events.

Ultimately, the requirement for a process-based platform should support executable business processes, business events, and business decisions as defined by an ongoing evolution of business operations. As mentioned in the introduction, requirements gathering in business process management involve the three business metaphors: business processes, decisions, and business events. These metaphors are the mechanisms that drive system changes and allow systems to accomplish a high level of dynamic interaction. Some of the expertise will be technical, and some is business, but all are model driven.

In the new world of collaboration between the business units and IT, the business processes, events, decisions, and business rules will be supported and maintained visually and expressed as BPMN/DMN. Moving forward, organizations need to model their operational processes using a combination of process models in BPMN and decision models in DMN. Combining process-, event-, and decision-centric thinking in a linked set of models makes for easier management, a more agile organization—and enables organizations to meet their intended goals.

COMMERCIAL INFORMATION

INTRODUCTIONS

These are the companies that we recognize as leaders in the fields of Business Process Management and Decision Management. The information is provided for your use. If you are looking for training, solutions, integrations, or consulting, the companies and individuals will provide great assistance.

BLACK PEARL DEVELOPMENT

Black Pearl Development specializes in helping companies create process and decision-oriented solutions in complex engineering, energy, manufacturing, and financial domains. A comprehensive approach that starts with an architectural framework and includes Process, Event, and Decision modeling is the backbone of Black Pearl Development's approach for developing requirements. Our complete set of integration and development capabilities, including near shore resources, eases implementation and ensures rapid success.

Solutions for the Internet of Things

The Internet of Things will be a critical strategy for every business that must adapt to a newly transformed customer relationship, boost competitive advantage and generate new revenue streams. However, many factors go into creating compelling IoT offering—from product architecture, and wireless connectivity decisions, to security, analytics, billing, and go-to-market strategy—can make it a daunting undertaking. Today, many different means enable communication between the tiers of an IoT solution. Furthermore, existing solutions do not address the scalability requirements for a future Internet of Things; Black Pearl Development helps companies architect and build the IOT solutions that companies need.

Cloud computing has a large impact on IoT solutions and can provide for the "big data" capabilities demanded by those solutions. Traditionally, the ability to deal with very large amounts of data required a lot of computing power and has been very cost-prohibitive for businesses to access. This kind of processing power is needed in order to enable the type of business intelligence and decision analytics needed for IoT solutions, due to the sheer amount of data being generated on the edge devices. Because of the ability to allocate more resources instantaneously to an application, it is possible for a cloud solution to easily surpass the capabilities of a single organization's IT infrastructure. The cloud also provides more agility because of the ability to bring up infrastructure and applications very quickly. With this increased agility, organizations can expand or adapt to changing market conditions, such as needing to address the evolving IoT world, with less risk and at less cost.

Contact Us

www.blackpearldevelopment.com

info@blackpearldevelopment.com

+1 (540) 817-4304

DECISION MANAGEMENT SOLUTIONS

DECISION MANAGEMENT SOLUTIONS

Decision Management Solutions specializes in helping companies build decision-centric, action-oriented systems and processes using decision management, business rules, and advanced analytic technologies. Decision modeling is the cornerstone for developing requirements for these next-generation systems and processes. Our consulting, training, and software eases implementation and ensures success.

Consulting
Decision Modeling

- Decision Modeling Service
- Requirements Conversion
- Existing Implementation Modeling
- Decision Inventory

Decision Management

- Decision Management System Design
- Vendor Selection
- Rapid Kickoff Service
- Decision Requirements Modeling Service

Business Rules

- Getting Started
- Vendor Selection
- Center of Excellence

- Implementation Best Practices
- Re-platforming strategy

Predictive Analytics

- Getting Started
- Vendor Selection
- Business Understanding Definition
- From BI to Analytics Strategy and Roadmap

Training and Workshops

- Live online training in Decision Management and Decision Modeling (an IIBA Endorsed Course)
- Live online and on-site training with BPMInstitute.org
- Online course
- Defining Business Goals for Predictive Analytics - University of California, Irvine Extension
- On-site workshops in Decision Modeling and Decision Management

Decision Modeling Software—DecisionsFirst Modeler

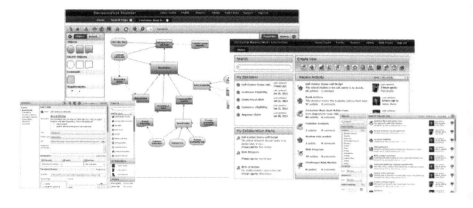

Our collaborative decision modeling software, DecisionsFirst Modeler, is based on the new Decision Model Notation (DMN) standard.

Key Features

- Interactive decision diagrams allow each decision to be decomposed, showing exactly how each decision is made, how it can be improved, and what rules, analytics, and data are needed.
- A shared repository provides a framework for managing business rules, checking completeness, and managing reuse.
- Decisions requirements are a common language across business, IT, and analytic organizations improving collaboration, increasing reuse, and easing implementation.

More details on DecisionsFirst Modeler are available at:
http://decisionmanagementsolutions.com/decisionsfirst-modeler.

What Our Clients Are Saying

- "This is the critical path to monetizing advanced models."—*Head of Analytics, North American Insurance Company*
- "Concrete, actionable recommendations."—*Program Leader for Next Best Action Program at a top European Retail Bank*
- "What used to be one week of requirements work was done in a few hours with decision management."—*Lead Business Analyst at a top Insurance Company*

Vendor Services

Decision Management Solutions also offers services to software and consulting firms:

- Strategic advice on product strategy, roadmap, and development.
- Independent validation of solutions and product reviews.
- Independent substantiation of the power of Decision Management to improve technology applications.
- Evangelism, independent research, and promotional services, such as white paper writing, to support adoption of Decision Management and its related technologies.

Speaking and Keynotes

Decision Management Solutions is led by leading decision management expert James Taylor. James is an experienced keynote presenter, speaking on analytics, decision management, business rules, and more. James is passionate about helping companies adopt Decision Management to develop agile, analytic, and adaptive business processes and systems. He has spent the last 20 years developing approaches, tools, and platforms that others can use to build more effective information systems.

James is also the author of "Decision Management Systems: A Practical Guide To Using Business Rules And Predictive Analytics" (IBM Press, 2011), "Smart (Enough) Systems: How to Deliver Competitive Advantage by Automating Hidden Decisions" (Prentice Hall) with Neil Raden, and has contributed chapters on Decision Management to multiple books including "Applying Real-World BPM in an SAP Environment," "The Decision Model," "The Business Rules Revolution: Doing Business The Right Way," and "Intelligent BPM Systems: Impact and Opportunity," as well as many magazine articles.

Contact Us

www.decisionmanagementsolutions.com

info@decisionmanagementsolutions.com

+1 (650) 400-3029

BPMINSTITUTE.ORG

BPMInstitute.org is the largest practitioner-led community of BPM professionals in the world, with over 60,000 members.

Member services include training and certification, BPM events, a wide range of vendor-neutral BPM and related content, as well as face-to-face and online networking.

Industry experts

The content includes works from industry experts and thought-leaders that deal with holistic management and aligning all aspects of an organization with the wants and needs of clients. It also promotes business effectiveness and efficiency while striving for innovation, flexibility, and integration with technology.

The knowledge you need

BPMInstitute.org gives you the flexibility to learn what you need to successfully lead your company's transformation to a more efficient, process-centric organization. BPMInstitute.org training, events, and collaboration allow you to:

- Gain proficiency in concepts and principles of proven disciplines and methodologies
- Learn how to incorporate state-of-the-art tools and techniques
- Avoid pitfalls and leverage successes of models from real-world case studies

View all Training Courses at www.BPMInstitute.org/training

Earn your BPMP—or just take a course or two

Whether you are interested in working toward a BPMP^{SM} Certificate or just want to take individual courses to brush-up on the latest developments in the field, you have access to the training you need online, on-demand, or face-to-face.

Learn more about BPMP^{SM} Certificate:
www.bpminstitute.org/training/certificate-training

Certify your BPM proficiency—become a CBPMP

BPMInstitute.org's Certified Business Process Management Professional (CBP-MPSM) program supports the advancement of BPM professionals by providing a way to measure and document the knowledge and skills required to be recognized as a competent practitioner. CBPMP certification helps employers define job objectives, evaluate position candidates, assess employee performance and motivate employees to enhance their skills and knowledge. CBPMPs enhance their professional experience by obtaining recognition of their competency, and proving that they are professionally qualified to practice their profession.

Let everybody know you've achieved that mastery with a CBPMPSM certification from the industry's top BPM educational organizations.

Learn more about CBPMP^{SM} Certification:
www.BPMInstitute.org/certification

Contact Us

www.BPMInstitute.org

info@BPMInstitute.org

+1 (508) 475-0475, x15

SALIENT PROCESS

Salient
Process
Your process. Our passion.

Salient Process is a premier provider of BPM expertise from Strategy to Execution. Our leadership team has over 50 + years of BPM experience and knowledge. We have enabled successful Process implementations across many industries such as Energy, Retail, Banking, and Insurance. Our services focus on helping our clients mature from BPM projects to developing transformational programs.

Our business transformation services align people, processes, and technology to enable innovative thinking, operational improvements, and value maximization. We deliver process excellence and experience across all of an enterprise's process needs by performing a range of Process Strategy Services. These services include Process Discovery and Modeling, Process Measurement and Analysis, Process Improvement, Aligning Process Performance with Business Strategy, and developing a plan to adopt Process Transformation across the enterprise.

Salient Process helps our customers move from Strategy to Execution. We have a strong team of Process consultants that use Business Process Management Suite (BPMS) and Business Rules technology to develop process-aware business applications to meet your business requirements. Our application development methodology blends Agile best practices to iteratively model, analyze, develop, and improve each phase of the business transformation process. Where a process-based solution is required, we heavily engage with the business stakeholders to incorporate their feedback and recommendations into each short development iteration.

Our sales specialist team is eager to better understand your business requirements and provide some options where we can partner together. Our goal is to be your strategic business partner for business transformation with BPM.

Contact Us

www.salientprocess.com

info@salientprocess.com

+1 855.4.SALIENT (855.472.5436)

OBJECT MANAGEMENT GROUP® (OMG®)

The Object Management Group® (OMG®) has been guiding the standardization of Business Process Modeling for the past decade. In particular, it adopted the Business Process Model & Notation (BPMN) specification which provides a graphical notation for specifying business processes in a Business Process Diagram. The specification's goal is to support BPM by providing a standard notation that is comprehensible to business users yet represents complex process semantics for technical users. More information on the specification can be found at www.bpmn.org.

The OMG BPMN Model Interchange Working Group works to ensure the smooth interchange of BPMN models between tools that implement the standard. The group's interchange test framework helps tool providers iron out any wrinkles in their exchange as well as identify any ambiguities in the standard.

In addition to the BPMN standard, OMG offers a certification program for BPM practitioners. Credentials are important in the BPM world, where practitioners may work on many projects for different clients over time. Holders of the OMG's Certified Expert in BPM 2 (OCEB 2) certificate show they have the knowledge, skills and commitment required in their profession. An OCEB 2 certificate can open the door to job advancement and promotion. More information can be found at www.omg.org/oceb-2.

Celebrating its 25th anniversary in 2014, OMG is an international, open membership, not-for-profit technology standards consortium. OMG Task Forces develop enterprise integration standards for a wide range of technologies and an even wider range of industries (including healthcare, finance, and automotive). OMG's modeling standards enable powerful visual design, execution and maintenance of software and other processes. Visit www.omg.org for more information on BPMN and other OMG technology standards.

INDEX

Made in the USA
San Bernardino, CA
26 January 2016